CHAIN SAW CONFIDENTIAL

HOW WE MADE THE WORLD'S
MOST NOTORIOUS HORROR MOVIE

GUNNAR HANSEN

CHRONICLE BOOKS

SAN FRANCISCO

Library of Congress Cataloging-in-Publication Data

Hansen, Gunnar, 1947–
  Chain saw confidential : how we made the world's most notorious horror movie /
Gunnar Hansen.
      pages cm
  Includes bibliographical references and index.
  ISBN 978-1-4521-1449-1
1. Texas chain saw massacre (Motion picture) 2. Hansen, Gunnar, 1947– 3. Motion
picture actors and actresses—United States—Biography. I. Title.

PN1997.T4265H36 2013
791.43'72—dc23

2013014844

MANUFACTURED IN CANADA

DESIGNED AND TYPESET BY LYDIA ORTIZ

10 9 8 7 6 5 4 3

Chronicle Books, LLC
680 Second Street
San Francisco,
California 94107
www.chroniclebooks.com

for Betty

The less said about Tobe Hooper's
The Texas Chain Saw Massacre the better

—David Robinson, *The Times* of London,
November 19, 1976

CONTENTS

INTRODUCTION

Once upon a time in 1973 some college students in Texas decided to get together at a friend's farm and make a movie. They had never made one, but they figured it would be fun. And if they did it right, they would all get rich. Especially if they made a film of the horrific story that had been in all the Texas papers—a series of killings and mutilations by a cannibal family near Corsicana, Texas, that had been exposed only days before, when a victim escaped her would-be killers. (There are those today who say one killer escaped and *is still out there*.)

With this story in hand, the filmmakers got some mob money, slapped together an outline, and called it *Stalking Leatherface*. They could work out the script's details, they figured, as they went along. Then they found a bunch of acting students itching to get rich, too.

Unfortunately, nothing went right during the shooting. Everyone was incompetent and people hated each other. Most were so stoned that later they remembered only that they had had a lot of fun. The sensitive-poet teenager playing the lead killer suffered terrible psychological damage from his role; he couldn't act, so the director cut all his lines and put a mask on him.

Neighbors complained about disturbing events at the farmhouse. The police came. People died. No one wanted their name on the credits. The film was an inept, blood-soaked disaster. The director had to prove to the FBI that it was not a snuff film.

Everyone hated the movie when it came out, except for a few perceptive academics who could see past the chain saw to recognize allegorical echoes of both the corrupting influence of the Viet Nam war and the collapse of the American family. Oh, and also bourgeois sexual repression.

Then everyone got rich, and they lived happily ever after.

And that is how *The Texas Chain Saw Massacre* became the Mother of All Splatter Movies.

———•———

None of this is true.

But if we pasted together all the tales and rumors about *Chain Saw*, this is roughly the story we would end up with. It is the accumulated myth of the making of *The Texas Chain Saw Massacre*, one of the most notorious, reviled, and beloved horror movies ever made.

So let's set the story straight.

There are a lot of questions to be addressed: Why is *Chain Saw* so controversial? How did it enter the culture? How has it influenced other movies? How could it become such a landmark movie? Why is it so successful as a horror movie and yet so hated by many mainstream film and social critics? And why did these myths attach themselves to this movie?

To answer these questions, or try to, we must go back to *Chain Saw*'s beginnings. So let's talk about how this movie got made, who made it, what happened on the set day to day, and how the actors and crew survived it. Let's talk about what these filmmakers were trying to do, what they expected, and what they ended up with—and why. Let's talk about what the critics and audiences said about the movie when it was released and how that reception has evolved over the years.

Let's talk about what has made this movie what it is, what horror is, what horror movies are, and how *Chain Saw* fits into that puzzle. Let's talk about why some people dismiss it as a bunch of crap, others consider it the greatest horror movie ever made, and still others blame it for everything that is wrong with American society and, of course, the corruption of its children.

The reason I want to talk about this movie is that I played Leatherface, *Chain Saw*'s brutish, relentless—yet apparently lovable—killer. Through an improbable series of events, one sweaty summer afternoon I found myself dancing on a Texas hilltop, spinning a chain saw over my head, hell-bent on scaring the bejesus out of the director. It had been a long trip getting to that hilltop, and it has been a long trip since.

I remember the filming. Unlike many of those who claim to have been involved with *Chain Saw*, I was actually there. And I have had plenty of time to gather my thoughts about what happened and about the significance of *The Texas Chain Saw Massacre*.

Telling the "true" *Chain Saw* story is a bit like being a character in Kurosawa's *Rashomon*—each player has his or her own take on what happened and what it means. And each of us has an emotional interest in remembering the story a certain way. A *Chain Saw* crew member once told a writer, "I happen to know the truth—whatever anybody says, that's fine, but I happen to know the truth." Really? I have also heard other *Chain Saw* actors tell stories about what I did on set that couldn't possibly be true. Could they?

Memory is a bit flexible, but while each of us remembers the same event differently, I know *I'm* right most of the time. And when we remember something, we really don't remember the event itself. We remember the last time we remembered the event; a psychologist once told me that. You can see how that hall of mirrors leads to a kind of infinitely regressing truth, never quite visible but somewhere in the background of *that* mirror—or is it *this* mirror?

Let's say, then, that this is what I remember of how it went, reinforced by conversations with many of those other cast and crew members who were there when we made the world's most notorious horror movie. Maybe the truth will lie somewhere among these stories.

Besides, someone has to explain what happened.

CHAPTER 1

WHAT HAPPENED IS TRUE

Call me Leatherface. Some years ago—never mind how long precisely—having little or no money in my purse and nothing particular to interest me otherwise, I thought I would do a little acting and see how movies are made. Every once in a while, when the world gets to be too much and I start to feel a bit spleeny, I feel the need to lift my spirits by killing someone. Whenever I find myself involuntarily pausing before coffin warehouses and bringing up the rear of every funeral I meet, I know it's high time to get onto a horror movie set to harmlessly act out my impulses.

Besides, I needed a job and I thought this would be an interesting one. How many people can tell their friends that they were once in a horror movie, even some obscure thing no one ever heard of?

Still, considering my personality, it was curious that I had decided to be in a movie. I had always hated performing in front of strangers, or even just standing in front of my classmates. In kindergarten, the school Christmas play had left me sweating in fear. Worse, I had muffed my one line. "There was no room at the inn" became "There was no room at the hotel."

As those words floated out into the audience, I desperately wanted to disappear. My brother's chums unkindly reminded him that we were related. And I will forever know that somehow a hotel is not quite an inn, though my dictionary is mum on the difference.

My fear of visibility stayed with me over the years, so in high school I joined the debate team to confront it. That helped a bit. But not enough.

By the time I was in graduate school at the University of Texas, in Austin, I was writing poetry and taking part in readings. That meant I had to stand up in front of people and perform. Most of us would-be poets were really bad at it. None of us knew how to present our work or ourselves in a way that engaged the audience. And I was the worst—I knew that just the fearful quaver in my voice would drive people out of the room. So I decided once again to do something about it. I took a poetry performance class.

Unfortunately (it seemed to me at the time) my professor liked my voice, so she gave me some additional work. I would not get my grade, she said, unless I acted in some of her directing students' plays. I had no choice. First I played a series of characters in a Mark Twain pastiche. From there I went on to *Of Mice and Men*, in which I played Lennie Small, the brutish giant who accidentally kills a puppy. And then—well, he does some more killing.

A year later, fresh out of grad school and freshly fired as a bartender, I ran into the actor who had played George to my Lennie. We found a table at a local joint near the university campus for a cup of coffee.

A friend of his joined us to listen in on our reminiscences. Eventually he asked me if I was an actor.

I mumbled something noncommittal.

It was too bad that he hadn't met me earlier, he said. Some guys in town were making a horror movie. He had a role in it himself, and I would have been perfect as the killer—except the part had already been cast. He did not explain why I would have been perfect. I didn't think anything of it.

Some days later I ran into him on the street. He was excited to see me again. The situation had changed, he said. The filmmakers were looking for a killer after all, because the original actor was holed-up drunk in a motel and wouldn't come out. He gave me the name and number of the casting director.

What part was he himself playing, I asked.

He smiled sheepishly. He wouldn't be in the movie, he said. He had backed out. Bad karma, he said, being in a movie like that. Bad for the soul.

I don't even remember his name. But I have often wondered what happened to him and what he thought in later years of having quit the film. I have also asked Kim Henkel, *Chain Saw*'s co-writer and associate producer, who he might have been. Kim does not remember that a cast member quit before production started, or even that they had cast a Leatherface before me. Maybe this mysterious character was just some ghost haunting the docks before this production set sail for its fate.

The casting director turned out to be Robert Burns. I had known of Bob in high school, though he had graduated the year before I arrived. He had been part of the drama club and often stage-managed productions, as well as designing and constructing sets. He had a reputation for his droll sense of humor and had been so popular with his drama club mates that he had come back the next year to visit. That is when I heard of him. By that time he was writing for *The Texas Ranger*, the University of Texas humor magazine, the highest achievement I could imagine. Eventually he would become its editor.

A decade later, Bob still had that dreadful sense of humor, larding his talk with agonizing, improbable puns delivered with a stretched-out Central Texas drawl and an expectant pause at the end, as if waiting for a groan. Now he was in a storefront office in downtown Austin, doing promotional design. He called his business The Rh Factor, a bloody name honoring Rondo Hatton, a B-movie actor of the 1930s and 1940s who had suffered from gigantism. Hatton had played villains in a series of thrillers, including *The Brute Man* (1946), in which he played, of course, "The Brute Man." Bob had proclaimed himself "the world's greatest, and only," living Rondo Hatton expert.

A Linda Lovelace *Deep Throat* pinball machine dominated the small Rh Factor office, something Bob had designed and built from a previously defunct, more innocent machine. He was proud of his invention and quick to point it out. It eventually appeared in *Playboy*.

In fact, the office was cluttered with debris, mostly props for the new movie—cowhides and bones and strange lamps and balsa-and-foam sledgehammers and fake wrenches. Apparently Bob was handling the casting only on the side. His real job was as the movie's art director and production designer. His main worry right then, he said, was whether to dress the set with a plastic skeleton or a real one. Human bones, available from India, were much cheaper than the plastic. It was a common movie dilemma, money versus ethics.

Our conversation was brief. The movie was called *Leatherface*, he said, and they were looking for someone to play a crazed killer who wore a mask throughout the movie. Was I interested?

I said yes.

He said he would call me.

I doubted that he would. To me, "We'll call you" sounded a lot like "We won't call you."

But Bob did call. Could I come down to meet the director and the writer?

I headed downtown immediately. Though I still dreaded performing in front of an audience, this was different. It was a movie, and if I made a mistake on camera we would just shoot it again. Besides, I had already killed on stage and knew I could do it again. And I needed a summer job.

Director Tobe Hooper and his co-writer, Kim Henkel, were waiting for me. Tobe had a mop of brown hair hanging across his forehead, a thin beard, and half a dead panatela in his mouth.

The dark-haired Kim was more gaunt and somewhat taciturn, but friendly enough. As I remember, Tobe did most of the talking.

Had I done any movie work before, he asked. Well, I said, I had been in a couple of student films, but I was a quick learner. He frowned. I took it that student films didn't count and it would be best not to talk about that. This was real filmmaking—hard and bloody work.

We spent the next hour or so discussing the plot of their new movie, Leatherface's personality and mental state, and his relationship to his family. At least I remember it was an hour—Kim says it was a relatively short and vague conversation, considering how much they needed to tell me.

Long meeting or short, Tobe explained that Leatherface—I loved the idea of having the title role—was retarded. (There is a new term these days, "developmentally challenged." Or maybe we would now call Leatherface "differently abled." But at the time "retarded" was perfectly acceptable.) In fact, Leatherface was so retarded that he didn't really talk, though he did grunt and squeal like a pig at times. Could I squeal like a pig?

I would learn, I said.

Tobe added that Leatherface was insane in a way that made him unpredictable and extremely violent. All this made for a very dangerous man.

The family dynamic was also quite screwed-up, with one vicious, scheming brother (the Hitchhiker); a violent older brother (the Cook) who desperately wanted to think of himself as respectable; and a hundred-and-eight-year-old patriarch (Grandpa) who had long since slipped into a kind of infantile stupor, but whom the family held in awe. As ferocious as Leatherface was, he was also deeply afraid of the others and would do whatever they told him to.

This household was entirely mad. And it lacked women. Still, Leatherface would fill in for this shortage now and then, not by dressing up in women's clothing, but by literally putting on their faces as masks.

Finally, after this detailed explication, Tobe asked me three questions.

"Are you violent?"

"No," I said.

He paused. "Are you crazy?"

"No. Not the way you mean it."

He frowned. Clearly these were not the answers he had hoped for. "Well, do you think you can do it?"

"Sure," I said. "It'll be easy."

He smiled and sat back. I had the part.

I was relieved. I really wanted to play Leatherface.

In the end it all had come down to these three questions. And though the first two made me wonder what Tobe thought acting was all about, I was delighted to know that I would be playing this retarded, insane, brutal character. I was excited to be in a movie, of course, so maybe my delight simply came from being thought good enough to do it. As to whether I could actually play Leatherface effectively, I had no idea. I would worry about that later. Right now I would just shake hands with Tobe and Kim and enjoy the thrill of having been cast.

———◦———

The thrill ended quickly when I began to think about the realities. They became unavoidable when I went to the contract party a few days later, something I had never heard of before. It was not a party. It was a serious gathering at someone's apartment, where we signed contracts and worked on costuming. Tobe was there, as was Kim. It was here that I met some of the other actors and crew and we were fitted for our costumes.

I brought some shirts and my old cowboy boots—I was a big guy with size fourteen feet, and I knew I would be hard to fit. Tobe chose an old, striped, short-sleeved shirt, saying that the wardrobe people would dye the shirt to tone it down and also replace the boots' worn out soles.

Makeup woman Dottie Pearl (wife of *Chain Saw* cinematographer Daniel) looked me over and said that she would trim my long hair enough so that when she pulled it up into a kind of Sumo topknot, it would fit under my mask. And my beard would have to go. I hated losing that—I had grown it when I was eighteen years old, and eight years later was quite attached to it.

The other actors were going through the same process. Teri McMinn, playing Pam, who would meet her end on the meat hook, was staring at her very small outfit, including the shortest shorts I had ever seen. Teri had been my college roommate's girlfriend some years before. When we saw each other we both said the same thing: "What are *you* doing here?"

Bill Vail, playing Pam's boyfriend, Kirk, the first to die—from a couple of well-placed sledgehammer blows—was told he would sport a constant two-day beard for the duration of filming, which Dottie said she could manage with a daily pass of her electric clippers.

Allen Danziger was Jerry, the wisecracking van driver who would also meet a hammer, this time in the kitchen. Like me, and unlike the others, Allen had no long-term acting ambitions. He was a social worker and just thought the filming was a chance to try something new. He also had a distinct New York accent. When I asked him how he had come to Austin, he said that he had boarded the wrong train in the Bronx and ended up there, a story he still sticks to.

I do not remember whether Paul Partain was there—he who would play the whining, tiresome, wheelchair-bound Franklin with such constant, intolerable Method Acting conviction that I would relish carving him in half with the chain saw. It seems like he would have been there, but maybe quietly, not yet in excruciating character.

Marilyn Burns would play Sally, the only one of these friends to survive the chain saw family's onslaught. When handed her script, she quickly flipped through to find her first scene. She was horrified. Her character was described, she says, as "bubblegum, braless Sally." She wondered why they had not just gone ahead and added "blonde" to the description. She was told to buy herself a wardrobe—"tight" tank top and pants. The pants should be white so they would show up during the night filming. "I felt like I was already braless, bubblegum, blonde Sally," Marilyn says. "And now I was going to learn to be a slut."

I met these "victims" only briefly that night and, except for Teri, had little idea of who they were. I would also spend little time with them during the filming—they were kept separate from the killers as much as possible. At least on set I would have plenty of chances to stand back and watch them.

We were four in the family of killers. Jim Siedow, fifty-three at the time, was the Cook. (In the script he is "the Old Man," but we never called him that.) Jim was the real pro among the actors, the only one who already had his SAG card. During filming he would need no help shifting from avuncular to sadistic.

Ed Neal was the Hitchhiker. Though Tobe had given Ed his contract before the party, he had come to meet everyone.

I did not meet John Dugan, our Grandpa, till later, when the filming started. Like me, he would not speak on camera. And like me, he would wear a mask—in his case a sculpted appliance and heavy makeup that made his twenty-year-old's face look a hundred-and-eight.

I would be paid $400 for my two weeks of acting (which would stretch to four weeks). It wasn't much, Tobe admitted, so the producers had added a fraction of a percentage point of the profits to everyone's pay—just in case the movie made any money. As further compensation, we would have a big wrap party after the filming with all the production stills available so we could pick some good shots for our résumés.

The contract listed two tentative titles for the movie: *Headcheese* or *Leatherface*. I was hoping for *Leatherface*, of course. I wanted the title role.

I signed the contract, and Tobe handed me my script (which said "Leatherface," not "Headcheese," a good sign). He must have said something more to me at the time about my character, because directly beneath the title I wrote: "Leatherface—voice a little high-pitched. Sometimes breaks."

"You know," Tobe said, "I wanted to hire you when you arrived for the interview."

"Oh?" That sounded good.

"Yeah. You filled the door."

So much for my acting ability, I thought. But then maybe it was good that he did not have high expectations.

I took the script home and started flipping through the pages, looking for Leatherface. Finally on page fifty-two I found him: ". . . a huge, dark figure suddenly appears . . . a horrible leathery mask covering the face and hair. . . . There is a high-pitched pig-like squeal ending in a hysterical whinny as the powerful arm flashes downward." Then, two pages later, a bit more: "Leatherface is terrifyingly quick for so monstrous a man."

I was not sure what to make of him. He sounded big, mean, and animalistic, as I expected, but otherwise this did not give me much sense of Leatherface as a character. I figured I had best go back to the beginning and actually read the script.

The grim story unwound in front of me. Sally Hardesty and her brother, Franklin, travel with three friends in a stifling van to their grandfather's grave site, worried that it may have been vandalized, then drive on toward the abandoned family home. On the way they pick up a freakish hitchhiker who menaces them and cuts himself and then Franklin before they can kick him out of the van. When they stop at an out-of-gas gas station and ask for directions to the old Franklin place, the attendant warns them about messing around in old houses.

There are bad omens along the way—a slaughterhouse, a human tooth lying on the porch of a nearby house the group investigates. Even the horoscope looks bad. Then Leatherface appears, and the killing begins: by sledgehammer, meat hook, freezer, and chain saw. Leatherface pursues Sally through the woods almost endlessly, until she is brought home for dinner with the family, a chaotic, deranged household with its own kind of bickering. Sally escapes. More pursuit. Leatherface cuts his own leg with the chain saw. . . .

I did not think that this was going to be a great movie. Nor did I think it would be awful. I had no experience with movie scripts and no idea what something on the page would look like on the screen. (Forty years and twenty-five movies later, I still don't.) But I didn't care. I just wanted the experience of being in a movie.

Even so, this was not going to be fun to make. I hated the heat and I hated running.

Still, I had no qualms about playing the role. It did not bother me that I would play a horrific character in a homicidally insane family. Even considering the earlier drop-out cast member's concern about karma and his soul—it was the '70s, after all—I cared nothing about such things. Acting was not being. I knew that it was Leatherface who would be psychotic, not I, and that we would always be separate.

Curiously, Marilyn worried about this for me. She says that she had heard even before the contract party that I was a "sensitive poet and writer," playing a character I didn't want to be. Surely the movie would damage me. I have no idea who fed her this notion.

Still, my main concern was how I would play Leatherface. I began to understand what I was facing in portraying him, and that that was something to worry about.

The first and most obvious problem was the physicality of the role. I would be spending many nights running through the woods in Texas in the middle of summer. How would I survive the distance and the heat?

I was not scheduled to film for a couple of weeks, so I had some time to get into condition. I started walking in my neighborhood before dawn, but quickly tired of the dogs chasing me. So I found

developmentally disabled persons. My mother worked at a clinic there, and I had visited it now and then—I had even once applied for a job at the school to work with blind, emotionally disturbed, retarded children—so I knew my way around the campus. Its grounds were also open, and plenty of residents spent time outside.

I started wandering the grounds, watching people. I was looking for something I could not quite define—a posture, a way of holding myself, a way of moving, something that might in some way reflect Leatherface's mentality. So I walked. And watched. I picked up a gesture from one man, the way he held his arm bent at the elbow. I noticed the way another stood, some part of him always moving, the way a third tilted his head. I tried out these details and many others on myself. Some seemed to work for me, some not.

After several hours I had cobbled together a set of postures and gestures of some kind and was trying to bind them together into a coherent whole as I walked by myself on the grounds. They could not be just a bag of random tics, a bunch of unrelated refer-ences—they had to work in a unified way. They had to make sense. They had to *be* Leatherface. I found that the key to unifying the character was all in the gesture, the way I moved my right arm, pulling it toward to my chest. Then the body followed.

Finally, as I tested this new body, I saw two staff members walking toward me. It was time to bring out my inner Leatherface. I slipped into the posture I felt comfortable with—my arm pulled up slightly, my shoulders slouched, my pelvis tipped forward, forcing me into a shambling walk. I made my way awkwardly toward them. They looked at and through me with little interest. Clearly I was just another State School resident.

Maybe I *could* play Leatherface after all.

CHAPTER 2

MY FAMILY'S ALWAYS BEEN IN MEAT!

Okay, I lied. I told Tobe and Kim that, other than being in a couple of student films, I had no movie experience. That was not quite true. I was in a Mexican romance. I usually don't like to talk about it—not because I'm ashamed, but because the story is longer than my screen time.

It was the late 1960s. I was in college and for some unsavory reason was wandering the streets of San Antonio. It was night. As I passed the St. Anthony Hotel I saw a film crew at its entrance with lots of bright lights. I joined the crowd to watch. A Beautiful Couple with black hair and clear skin pulled up in a white Cadillac convertible as the crew filmed their arrival.

The director yelled "Cut!" or the Spanish equivalent. There was a pause. He looked through the crowd. He spotted me. He motioned me over. "Can you walk from here to there without looking at the camera?" He pointed. I nodded. "Okay. Please do that when I call 'Action.'"

The action started. The Beautiful Guy opened the door of the white Cadillac convertible for the Beautiful Girl, and the Beautiful Couple entered the hotel. I crossed through the scene. I never looked at the camera.

A star was born.

That said, almost every other person involved with *Chain Saw* had more movie and acting experience than I.

Tobe, Kim, and Bob Burns already knew each other, as did many other participants. Like most of the crew, Tobe had worked on documentaries and TV commercials. He was famous locally for a film about folksingers Peter, Paul and Mary (*The Song Is Love* [1970], aired often on PBS), and for his 1969 feature *Eggshells*, a hippie movie that Hooper has described as "a mixture of Andy Warhol's *Trash* and Walt Disney's *Fantasia*," and that *Chain Saw* boom operator Wayne Bell said "was dated the moment they were through shooting it."

Bob had served as art director and Tobe's close collaborator on *Eggshells*, though he is not credited. In a 2004 interview, Bob said that at the time of filming *Chain Saw* he had known Tobe for about eight years. So, as Bob explained, "when it came time to make *Chain Saw*, I was just the logical choice to design it."

Kim met Tobe on *Eggshells*, playing a character named Toes. (In the credits he appears under the *nom d'cinéma* Boris Schnurr.) He also collaborated with Tobe on the script, creating some of the characters. He is modest about his work and says, "I think everybody who was involved in that had some contributions to what was going on, because it evolved from day to day." Still, his contribution was substantial enough that he and Tobe talked about eventually developing another script. Years later they got together to kick around ideas and developed what would become *The Texas Chain Saw Massacre* (the genesis of which they would explain to me late one night, before we shot the scene in which I kill Franklin).

Eggshells' first assistant director, Lou Perryman, became *Chain Saw's* assistant cameraman. He saved my life during the filming— often he was the only one who would talk to me, and we spent quite a few hours addressing the fundamental philosophical questions. No one wants to talk to the killer, so until the rest of the chain saw family arrived, I generally just sat by myself on set. But, when he could, Lou was happy to pass the time with me to break the tedium and ease my isolation. As for what these fundamental questions were, I now have no idea, though at the time they seemed important.

Fresh out of high school, Wayne Bell had found a summer job at Film House, the small Austin production company where Tobe was based. Wayne came back to Film House after his first year of college and spent that summer helping finish *Eggshells*, including some sound work. So when it came time to put together a crew for *Chain Saw* (then called *Leatherface*), Tobe asked Wayne to serve as boom operator, whose job was to get the mic as close as possible to the on-camera actors without being on camera itself. He had no training in this, and so would learn on the job. Wayne also recorded the postproduction sound effects and composed the score with Tobe—all crucial to *Chain Saw*'s success.

Allen Danziger, who had some screen time in *Eggshells*, would go on to *Chain Saw* as the wisecracking van driver, Jerry. Tobe and Kim brought him the script and offered him the part without his having to audition. He felt it was quite an honor to be asked since, he admits, he was "not an actor or anything like that." In fact, he had earned a degree in social psychology at the University of Texas and at the time of the filming was working at a camp for mentally retarded, socially disadvantaged kids. He read the script in two hours and wanted the part. "It fascinated me," he says. Still, he did not know what to expect. "There was stuff there that I didn't know anything about. In fact I think the scariest part for me was in the opening scenes where it had to do with [the dialogue about] the stars and the horoscope. I didn't know a Capricorn from a unicorn, so I didn't know how to read those lines."

John Dugan was not part of *Eggshells*, but his sister was married to Kim Henkel. At the time Kim asked John to play Grandpa, John was working in theater in Chicago, "dancing around in tights, entertaining children," as John puts it. Their conversation sounds familiar.

"He asked me if I was crazy," John says. "I said, 'Of course, Kim, you know me. Of course I'm crazy. Why?' 'Because I want you to do something crazy. We're making a little movie down here and I want you to play a role in it.'"

John put in his notice at the children's theater and two weeks later was in Texas, getting a cast made of his face to make him look one-hundred-and-eight years old. All this without seeing a script. (Even today, he doesn't think he has ever seen a complete one.)

Another movie figured in *Chain Saw's* creation, *The Windsplitter*, a low-budget counterculture motorcycle picture that was shot in 1970 in Columbus, Texas, eighty miles southeast of Austin. Tobe had acted in it (as a bad guy), as had Jim Siedow, who would go on to play the Cook. Kim Henkel worked as a grip. Sallye Richardson, who became assistant director as well as an editor on *Chain Saw*, was the assistant director. (She was also one of Tobe's Film House gang.) Ron Bozman, *Chain Saw's* production manager, was key grip on *Windsplitter*. He had roomed with Kim in a motel in Columbus during the shoot. Most important to me, Ron was also our chain saw wrangler. Because of his good work, my saw always started on the first pull. He would go on to produce *The Silence of the Lambs* (1991).

Ron was also a technical advisor on *Lovin' Molly*, a big-time, big-name Hollywood picture directed by Sidney Lumet and shot near Austin in 1972. That movie also connected a number of people to *Chain Saw*. (Filmmaking is a disturbingly inbred business.) Paul Partain, who would go on to play Franklin, was working at an Austin dinner theater at the time and had been recommended for *Lovin' Molly* by his director, scoring a small part. This same director reportedly later connected Paul to Tobe and Kim, who at first considered Paul for the Hitchhiker. They were unimpressed with his reading and had him instead read for the part of Franklin and feed lines to the actors auditioning for the Hitchhiker. "So I sat there reading Franklin over and over and over again, and got to liking him," Paul said in a 2004 interview.

Marilyn Burns, a former University of Texas drama student who would play Sally in *Chain Saw*, was originally cast as a lead in *Lovin' Molly*, but was replaced at the last moment. "I did get costumed," she explains. "I got my script and everything, and then they called me and said, 'Well, Marilyn, you can't—the agents are packaging it. In order to get [Anthony] Perkins, Blythe Danner, and Beau Bridges, they are going to have this new girl called Susan Sarandon.' So they let me stand in for six-foot Blythe Danner and five-foot-seven Susan. Blythe was actually five-foot-seven. It just seemed she was six feet by the way she acted." Marilyn was five-two.

It was on *Lovin' Molly* that Marilyn met Tobe and Kim. They had sneaked onto to the set, likely invited out by Ron Bozman and maybe hoping to make some contacts. Marilyn knew about Tobe, she says, "as any young actress wants to know every filmmaker there is. He had just made *Eggshells*, and he had [a documentary on] Peter, Paul and Mary under his belt. So, yes, I kept my eye on him. Why not? So now we are acknowledging each other like we are great friends because we are the only Texans in the group." Ron was not on set that day. Had he been there, he says, he could have protected them from what happened next.

Tobe and Kim had decided to join the *Lovin' Molly* cast for lunch. They got in line and helped themselves to the chicken. But they were spotted, told to put the food back, and thrown off the set.

"I thought all was lost," Marilyn says.

But she was ambitious. At the time she was part of the newly formed Texas Film Commission, and when she heard there that Tobe and Kim were putting together a movie, she decided that she would try to get herself cast. She got the lead. She wasn't concerned by the subject matter, or that it was a horror film. In fact, she liked horror and was grateful for the chance. "I wanted it to be good," she says. "I believed in this movie from the beginning. I always thought it would work. I knew it was going to go in the theaters because I was starring in it, and I wanted to star in a movie." Still, she remained nervous throughout the filming, fearing that, even though she was the central character, somehow she would be cut in the final edit. "If I didn't get left on the cutting room floor, then I had a chance of starting my career properly."

The head of the Film Commission in those days was Warren Skaaren, who had been Ron's college roommate at Rice University. He would eventually leave the Commission and become deeply involved with the movie's ongoing life—including coming up with a new name, transforming it from *Leatherface* to *The Texas Chain Saw Massacre*. (He would also go on to a substantial movie career, including writing *Beetlejuice* (1988) and *Batman* (1989) before his death in 1990 at age forty-four.)

Austin was small then, especially the film community, and people of like mind got to know of each other quickly.

Daniel Pearl, Ted Nicolaou, and Larry Carroll had a small film production company in Austin called Shoot Out. Daniel shot film, Ted ran sound, and Larry edited. Daniel and Ted had been close friends all though college and were fresh out of grad school. Daniel, only twenty-three years old, had finished his master's degree in film at UT three weeks earlier. Still, by his own admission, he was pretty cocky. "I boldly made a statement," he says, "that I thought I was pretty good at this cinematography thing, and I figured I was going to shoot a movie by the time I was thirty-five. I would be the youngest guy ever to shoot a movie."

Shoot Out had recently finished a law-enforcement documentary that included some dramatic drug-bust footage. Though the cops apparently didn't like what they saw, Tobe did. (Film House and Shoot Out used the same film processing lab, where Tobe saw the footage.) Three weeks after Daniel's graduation, Tobe called.

"He said, 'I reckon I've seen some of your work, and I reckon you're the best cinematographer in Texas, so I want you to shoot this film,'" Daniel recalls. "He also said that he wanted a Texan to photograph this film. I didn't consider myself a Texan [Daniel grew up in northern New Jersey], but, boy, I sure changed my accent quickly as soon as he said that.

"I tried to play it a little bit cool, and I said, 'Sure, man, can I read the screenplay?' I hung up the phone and I was electrified. There must have been sparks coming off of me or something." Daniel's wife, Dottie, asked what was going on. "I said, 'I'm twelve years ahead of schedule. I've just been offered a movie!'

"He sent over the screenplay and, oh my God, it was all there on paper, really strong. It scared me just to read it. I wanted to do it. First of all, I was surprised that Tobe wanted to hire me. *I* wouldn't have hired me at the time. So, because I was worried that he would come to his senses, I wanted to get it going as soon as possible."

Tobe would also bring on Ted as sound recordist and Larry as editor, bringing the full complement of Shoot Out talent to *Chain Saw*. Asked when the shooting would start, Tobe said that they were ten thousand dollars short of having all the money. They had one investor, Jay Parsley, who was putting together the rest and would be the film's executive producer. But Parsley (known to some as Bill, his first name) did not want to be the only investor; he wanted to make sure other people believed in the movie, too. Once they had that additional ten thousand, they would start.

"I'm thinking, *Oh my God*," Daniel says, "Ten thousand dollars, in 1973 . . . I was living in a *house* that cost ten thousand dollars."

Then Daniel remembered an old college friend who engaged in "nefarious activities" and thus had a lot of cash lying around, and who—crucially—was a film buff. "So I rang him up and said, 'Listen, I've been offered this movie and I think it's pretty good. Would you care to read the screenplay? Because they're looking for an investor.' I brought the screenplay to him. Three hours later he rang back. 'I want in. How much money can I put in?' I got the ten thousand dollars in a shopping bag, and off we went to make the movie."

Tobe originally wanted twenty-year-old Dottie to play the part of Pam, but Dottie wanted to do makeup. Tobe was reluctant, saying "That's the one person that has to know what the hell they're doing in this movie." He was sure that the makeup person would come from Hollywood.

"I had to shoot some lens tests," Daniel says, "and I was shooting Dottie looking beautiful. Then she said, 'Hang on a second, let me do this horror job on myself.' She used the shell of an egg to make her eyeball appear to be dull. She used an apricot to fill in the eye socket. She somehow filled that in like she'd been beaten. She cut raisins down and made oozing scabs on her face, did quite a job on herself. And when Tobe saw her, he was so impressed she got the job."

Because of her *Chain Saw* work, Dottie became the first woman to join the Makeup Artist and Hair Stylist Guild, the Hollywood makeup union. The movie was to be her first step in a long, successful career.

Teri McMinn also got a phone call, one that would lead to her death on a meat hook. She was a drama student at St. Edwards University, a small school in south Austin, who wanted to be a working actor and took every role she could find. In the meantime she paid the bills waiting tables.

"I was doing a play," she says, "and [Tobe and Kim] saw my picture in the paper. Kim called and wanted to know if I would come and read for a horror movie. But you well know that at the time this was all happening, doing horror, hard-core horror, was like doing hard-core porn. And I'll be honest with you, I couldn't tell heads or tails from the script."

She tried out anyway. She had to start somewhere, and this was a start. The movie wrapped, she says, on her twenty-second birthday, August 18, 1973, although there's some debate about precisely when we started and wrapped filming. Curiously, this is also the date on the screen when the movie's story begins.

For all this small-world-of-film stuff, a few actors—like me— just heard about the movie and tried out. Ed Neal was a graduate student at the University of Texas Drama Department. He had been Bill Vail's roommate for a while in college, and they had worked in some plays together, but otherwise he knew no one involved in the movie. He was twenty-seven years old and had already served in the army in Viet Nam. He happened upon the casting call one day as he was coming out of acting class. When Tobe asked if he could "do weird," Ed channeled his schizophrenic nephew, and Tobe loved what he saw.

Bill, also a student in the UT Drama Department, had done some film work at the university's Radio, Television and Film Department, as well as a couple of jobs with local filmmakers. Though he was primarily a stage actor, he felt he would be better in film. "I heard this guy who had made *Eggshells*—which I had never seen, and still haven't seen—who was the local filmmaker, local-legend filmmaker, was getting together this horror movie and they needed some kids to kill. I thought, *I can do that.* I got Kim Henkel's phone number and called him up. We met on some doorstep somewhere in Austin and I brought my résumé and my little eight-by-ten, and we chatted. And then the next thing I knew, I was in the movie."

Bill originally wanted to play the wheelchair-bound Franklin. And though he was cast as Kirk, the first to die, he was still happy for the part.

"It was going to be my gateway to bigger and better things," he says. "I was just finishing school and had to decide where I was going to go. This was going to be a piece of work that I could take and show to people that I had done professionally. But past that, the movie was going to go into the drive-in theaters in Texas—and if it got out of Texas, I'd be surprised—and would die a slow death, and nobody would ever hear about it again."

Yeah, a lot of us thought that. Including me.

CHAPTER 3

STINKING TO HIGH HEAVEN

The first shot was to be of the sun, explosive flares and all, filling the frame. The sun image would dissolve to "the purple glazed eye of a dead dog," as the script reads. "Flies swarm the staring eye and the crackling noise becomes the buzzing of the flies."

It was art director Bob Burns's job to find the dog. He and his assistant (and girlfriend), Mary Church, eventually did find one. It lay in tall grass, its eyes open. The crew shot three takes, each starting with a close-up of the dog's eye, then pulling back to reveal the van pulling up in the background. In the last take a blowfly crawls over the dog's eye. Tobe did not use the shot, and it's no wonder why—it is heartbreaking. As Tobe once said of the decision, "Domesticated animals are too much."

Bob and Mary had also found a dead horse, but according to Bob it was "too icky," and it offended people's sensibilities.

Finally, they found the dead armadillo that would ultimately appear in the shot. Bob took it home, hoping to preserve it. "He got a do-it-yourself taxidermy book, and we stuffed that damned thing," Mary says. It was Bob's famous resourcefulness and his eye for macabre improvisation that became hallmarks of the unsettling and terrifying look he created for the film, and it was the armadillo—the symbol of funky, hippie Austin—that ended up as the roadkill omen for the kids in the van.

Fresh out of college with an English degree from the University of Texas and no film experience, Mary was also the production's script coordinator, whose job it was to track how scenes were shot and to make continuity notes. "I didn't have the faintest idea how to do that," she says, "but I was doing it nonetheless." She also became the production's only stunt person. She was everywhere, oftentimes literally jumping in when something needed to be done, a valuable talent in a low-budget, nonunion shoot with uncertain job boundaries and not enough people to otherwise get the work done. Like Bob, she was a quick learner, and in fact she still works in the film business today, as a production manager and producer in Hollywood.

"There really wasn't an art department other than us," Mary says. "So we pulled at least three twenty-four-hour days just between actually working on the set and then, either before or after, either dressing or undressing the set. After it finished, I thought, *I don't know if I can make it in the film business,* because it was so difficult. And of course it was hot Texas summer."

But Mary says that Bob, who died in 2004, loved working on *Chain Saw*. And a small budget of an independent production (reportedly an art budget of $3,000) did not bother him. "That was Bob's milieu. I mean, he was cheap. Virtually all the set came from thrift stores, and for a lot of the bones we scoured pastures. And so I don't think we recognized it as a hardship. In many ways this was our first real movie, and I don't think we thought twice about it. We just went shopping at Goodwill, and got what we got."

As an art director, Bob had certain quirks, which director Stuart Gordon discovered when working with Bob later on *Re-Animator* (1985). "One of the first things we talked about," Stuart explains. "I said, 'Would you do some drawings?' and he said 'I don't draw. No, I'm a terrible drawer,' which kind of took me aback, because this is a production designer and you kind of expect you're going to see some drawings. He said, 'The way that I do things is I kind of collect things.' And he started telling me about, on *Texas Chain Saw*, how he had gone to a slaughterhouse and gotten all these animal parts, pieces of bones, and hides, and all this stuff and used that as the basis for his design for that movie."

There was not much time to get ready for the shoot—three or four weeks, Mary recalls. But, as Tobe has said, overnight Bob could create another piece of "dead art." By the time he had finished dressing the set, Bob said in an interview at that time, "We used parts of eight cows, two dogs, a cat, two deer, three goats, two real human skeletons, one chicken, and an armadillo. There were only about ten plastic bones in the whole set."

"He was a brilliant production designer," Stuart Gordon adds, "and you couldn't get anybody better. He would always find something that was beyond the obvious. He'd come up with something, a real interesting, weird take on it that would just take it to the next level." Without Bob, *Chain Saw* would not be what it is. It is maybe a testament to the effectiveness of Bob's work that Tobe would later claim that he gave up eating meat during the filming, and that seeing *Chain Saw* was the reason that Guillermo Del Toro became a vegetarian. (Still, I never noticed that Tobe avoided the barbecue during lunch.)

And when it came to that skeleton for the set that Bob had been worrying about that first day I saw him in his office, I would like to remember that he bought the more expensive plastic one from the United States, but in his interview he claimed to have used *two* human skeletons. To be honest, it was inevitable. After all, Bob was cheap.

———•———

So the green Econoline van passes the stuffed armadillo, and we meet the young travelers off to meet their fate. Doomed kids in a van seems like such a horror cliché these days, but it was not so back then. They also sidestepped what would later become another cliché. "They're a little bit older than teenagers," Doug Bradley, "Pinhead" in the Hellraiser movies, says. "They're not smoking pot, they're not making out, they're not doing all the things you come to expect people in that situation are going to do and therefore get punished for."

Still, we all know they are going to get punished, whatever the reason. But first, wheelchair-bound Franklin has to pee. The van stops and Franklin, clutching a coffee can, rolls to the edge of a ditch. Then a gust of wind from a passing semi pushes the poor guy down the slope, and he tumbles to the bottom.

This was shot on Paul Partain's last day of filming. (A point of order: as with most movies, some parts of *Chain Saw* were shot out of story order. However, for the sake of clarity and my own sanity, I will follow the story as it unfolds.) In fact, Paul had his final paycheck in his pocket in this scene. The reason? Since this was to be his last day, he had asked for his pay beforehand so he would not get stiffed. The producers told him that there was no money, and they would like to defer his payment. Paul was not interested in this gladly-pay-you-someday business, so he refused to shoot the scene without first being paid.

Getting paid seems to be the eternal problem of low-budget filmmaking. John Dugan, playing Grandpa, ran into that problem himself, toward the end of the filming. Unfortunately, he had already shot his final scene when he asked for his pay. "They didn't have the money to pay me when they wrapped me out," he says. "'Oh, by the way, we can't pay you. There are a couple points available still.' I said, 'No, defer me, I want my money.' So I didn't get paid for a year, when the first box office started coming in." He was smart enough not to take percentage points in the future profits of the movie, which profits, as we'll see, would become a much bigger issue for everyone later.

Myself, I had no problems with pay while filming *Chain Saw*. But I was never paid for my role in my next movie, the laughably incompetent *The Demon Lover* (1977). I had been too naive to insist on being paid beforehand. I have been a bit more careful since then.

The shooting schedule allowed two days for the van scene, but actual shooting never seemed to fit the scheduled time. As sound recordist Ted Nicolaou says, every day the schedule fell further behind. It certainly felt like longer than two days. "It seemed like about six months," Bill Vail recalls.

Shooting in the van was a misery for the actors and the crew. It was July in Central Texas, with high humidity and temperatures hovering one side or the other of a hundred degrees every day. "Oh, so much fun in the van," Bill says. "Hot! Hot, hot, and hot! And stinky. Couldn't open a window because that would create sound problems, and so we're riding around all day, the eight of us. Cameraman, soundman, and Tobe, and then the five actors, in a totally closed van in the middle of Texas summer."

"I thought, *Well, can't they just cut the van in half like they do in the real movies and have a camera car?*" Ed Neal says. "Oh no, no, we don't have the money to get all that stuff." As such, with the van's middle seat ripped out and left by the side of the road somewhere (and never recovered), the actors took the space they needed for a specific shot, Ted squashed into the rear cargo area with his mixer on his lap, Daniel hunched over the camera, and Tobe crouched wherever he could be out of the shot.

"It's a hundred ten at least, and it feels like a hundred ninety in Texas, or worse," Marilyn says. "Your skin's hot. Your car's hot. You touch your seat, it's hot. Everything's hot. So we're all in this van, we are sweating profusely. Can't get the sound, can't get the camera. Actors blowing their lines . . . or we're not blowing our lines: we don't know what they are yet, because they keep changing them. It was just the heat, and the tension at the start of filming. And the armadillo. We were so miserable."

And then the Hitchhiker, Ed Neal, arrives, bringing the number of bodies in the van to nine. The other actors had not yet seen him in wardrobe and makeup.

"My line when we see him on the road, 'Oh, he looks weird,' was real," Teri McMinn says. "He *was* weird, he was just weird. I had not run into many other actors, so it was pretty wild filming with Ed. I thought he was the most freakazoid guy I had ever met in my life."

"Well, he definitely brought a real edge to what we were doing right away," Daniel says. "I mean, oh my God! This is the day and age before video assist, which meant that the only person who actually sees the exact shot is the cameraman himself. So as a cinematographer, what happens—especially when things are extremely interesting—is you almost leave your body and go into that machine, and you're just watching the movie no matter how uncomfortable or how hot or jammed you are. Ed's performance in there was certainly one of those moments."

Disturbingly manic and erratic, the Hitchhiker talks with Franklin about whether the best way to slaughter cattle is with a bolt gun or sledgehammer. The Hitchhiker shares some Polaroids he has taken of eviscerated carcasses, carries on about the delights of headcheese, shows off a straight razor he keeps in his sock, takes an instant photo of Franklin, and tries unsuccessfully to sell it to him for two dollars, at which point he ritually burns the picture with a flash of ignited gunpowder.

That did not go so well for the actors in the overcrowded van. "There wasn't a lot of direction," Ed says, "so the first time I did it, it was way too strong, and it almost blew us up."

"Come on, that was ridiculous," Marilyn says. "The very first time that we did the scene we thought there was an explosion in the van. Why didn't they get *that* shot? That would have been really good if they got that shot."

The first take spooked them enough that on the second try they used such a small load of powder that they had little more than a fizzle, but which still made the atmosphere in the van a bit more nasty. Ed says they got it right on the third or fourth take. Films with bigger budgets would have hired a pyrotechnician responsible for the explosives. "We were so young, so stupid, and so poor that we had to do everything in almost as realistic a way as possible," Marilyn says.

Still, this sort of low-budget semi-vérité added considerably to the weird but realistic feel of the film, and the burn—hard to shoot or not—was a shocker. Bob cited it as the kind of surrealism that is missing in other movies. The weirdness made the scene even creepier. It apparently was too creepy for Paul, who said that he never picked up a hitchhiker again.

All this is too much for the travelers. They throw the Hitchhiker out.

Before the five can drive off, the Hitchhiker smears his blood on the side of the van. I remember thinking at the time that it was supposed to be some kind of sign, as if to mark these kids for someone else to find, but that idea hardly goes anywhere, and it just ends up being an odd, creepy bit of business. It is not in the original script. In the shooting script, Sally sees the mark once they reach the gas station and says "That guy smeared blood on the van," but these are revised pages, likely written after Tobe told Ed to smear the blood. Later, when the travelers reach the old Franklin place, Kirk looks at the smear and says, "You think it's supposed to mean something?" Those shooting script pages are also revised.

In fact, Kim and Tobe revised lot of the script as the shooting went along. Looking at my copy of the shooting script, 38 percent of the pages are revisions, 62 percent are not. So of every five pages of script, two were revised. That seems like a lot to me, though ongoing script revisions while filming are certainly not unusual. "I think they were constantly reworking stuff," Allen says. "Something wasn't working and then they would come up with some new pages."

Often, at the beginning of each day, we would be given these new pages to replace some older ones, or we would be told which blocks of script to cross out. Sometimes parts were just rewritten in the middle of the shooting.

Lines were cut, even though they remained in the shooting script. For instance, most of the dialogue in the van before and after the Hitchhiker's arrival did not make it to the final movie. Sometimes entire scenes in the shooting script did not make it. An opening scene with locals at the graveyard before the kids arrive to check out their grandfather's grave and a scene when the kids leave the graveyard and discuss getting gas are gone. So is a scene before they reach the gas station in which they discuss which road to take. But these cuts make sense. Most of the missing material are unnecessary transitions, and without them the movie moves along more quickly.

"Most of it was paring down stuff that was excessive," Kim says. "I don't think we added a lot of dialogue from actors that was not in the script. I'm sure, like anything, there are bits and pieces here and there. There were some additional kinds of things. I would see opportunities and scribble on the back page of my script or a paper napkin. Like the Cook shouting 'Look what you did to the door!'—something like that. I don't know if it's in the actual script, but it's written by hand in my script."

It is interesting, too, that most of the revisions are in the first half of the script. Maybe as the shooting ground on, Tobe and Kim were too worn down to rethink everything. Or, more likely, as they had moved deeper into writing the original script, they got more sure of the material.

———

Many fans think the chain saw family's name is Sawyer, but it is not. They were given that name in the second *Chainsaw* movie in 1986. Their real name is Slaughter, as seen in faint letters on the sign above the gas station: W. E. Slaughter Barbecue. Bob made the sign. He said that Tobe and Kim were "mighty proud" of coming up with "we slaughter." Unfortunately, no one seeing the movie notices it. Kim did revive the Slaughter family name in his *Texas Chainsaw Massacre: The Next Generation* (1994), naming one of the characters W. E. Slaughter. (The gas station, by the way, was on a small road near Bastrop, east of Austin. For a while it was called Hills Prairie Grocery, then Bilbo's Texas Landmark.)

Once the travelers arrive at the gas station, they encounter the Cook/station attendant (played by Jim Siedow) and his helper, who is one odd character even for this movie, described in the script as "a dwarfish, moon headed man with idiot eyes."

"When I read the gas station scene," Marilyn says, "I remember saying, 'I have this friend in Dallas.' I called my friend, Robert Courtin, who was one of my best friends ever. He came down, and I knew Robert would be brilliant. He wasn't an actor, but he was a character." He fit the physical description perfectly, but he was not exactly as he seemed.

"He did have something physically wrong, something misshapen with his head at birth," she says. "But he was sharp as a tack and that's what was devious about him, too. Because he looked one way and was smart enough to shut up."

Robert provided the first light moments in the film, and in the shooting itself, slouching back and forth with his pail and rag, slopping and almost cleaning the van's windshield and lights. It looks like Robert was just ad-libbing, filling the time imaginatively while he waited for Jim to walk away, but he was following the script closely.

"He spreads soapy water on the windshield," Allen says, "and inadvertently I hit the windshield wiper, and it throws just a big glob of soapy water on Jim Siedow's face, and it's dripping down from him—I'm laughing, still—as he's still trying to deliver his lines. And I'm done. You could put a fork in me."

The tension and tedium and discomfort of the van finally dissolved in hilarity. For almost everyone.

"Jim got mad because he had all his makeup on, his hair all fixed, and his perfectly pressed little outfit, and probably we didn't have another one," Marilyn says. "We just had to let it sit in the sun for two minutes."

"Take two, the guy came out there," Bill says, "and then all he had to do was pick the rag up out of the bucket, and Allen and I lost it. I mean he would just put it on the windshield, never got close to Jim again, take six, take eight, whatever it was. Tobe got so fucking mad at us. 'Stop laughing!' And then the madder he got, the more hysterical we thought it was. I mean the whole thing—it was just one of those things. I felt like I was back with my brother in the back seat of the Chevy station wagon and we got the giggles."

Tobe never lost his temper again. But then, this was the only time we actually laughed at what was going on.

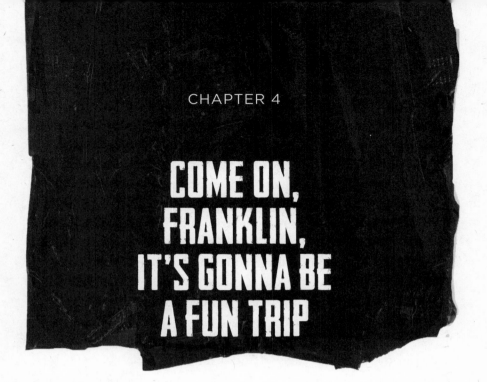

CHAPTER 4

COME ON, FRANKLIN, IT'S GONNA BE A FUN TRIP

My first day on set I just watched. I was not due to start filming for several days and had come out to see what making a movie was like. Our hapless travelers were at the old Franklin place. The long-empty house was north of Austin, just across the border in Williamson County, on the now abandoned Quick Hill Road. Interestingly, the chain saw family house was directly across the road, though in the film it is somewhere deep in the scrub brush on the opposite side of the Franklin place. In the late 1990s the chain saw family house was moved sixty miles west to Kingsland, where it was restored and opened as a restaurant, of all things. (I had a great steak there once. The restaurant closed in July, 2012.)

Although my copy of the production schedule does not show this to be the actual first day of filming, the consensus is that it was. As with most films, there was a lot of waiting. "We spent most of our time that day sweating and reapplying makeup," Marilyn says. "Then we'd sit in the sun and the people that were running the show were in the corner talking and making up their minds what the next shot was going to be."

Many of the cast and crew were feeling out their roles, including boom operator Wayne Bell. His microphone sometimes would creep into a shot. "This happens," cinematographer Daniel Pearl says. "And this happens certainly to us, a bunch of guys sort of figuring out how to make films on our own. So the camera is pointed down the staircase, wide-angle lens. Tobe sits down behind the camera, got the Dr Pepper in his right hand, cigar in his left hand. He puts his eye down on the camera. He goes, 'Daniel! Daniel! Goddamn it! The shot's brilliant, but the goddamn microphone is in the shot again. Only this time the son of a bitch is on fire!' It was his cigar; he was holding his cigar [within the view of the lens]."

In reality Tobe was easy to work with. In the first scene of that first day of shooting, Wayne noticed that his microphone actually was in the shot. He called "Cut!" and pulled the mic out. Tobe quietly took him aside and explained that it was not for him to stop a shot. Only the director could do that. "He was very kind, Tobe," Wayne says.

Once the travelers reach the old Franklin place, the two couples go upstairs, leaving Franklin alone in his wheelchair below. He struggles to get onto the porch, where he finds eerie, ritualistic bone-and-feather constructions, as if someone else has been there. Upstairs, Kirk wanders off on his own and finds a swarm of daddy longlegs high on one wall. Meanwhile Sally, Jerry, and Pam are in the old nursery, where they look at the zebra wallpaper and Sally reminisces about her childhood.

I stood in the background and thought how god-awful the dialogue was.

"This scene is so bizarre because there is no [scripted] dialogue," Allen Danziger once said. "They said 'Just make up your own gibberish.'"

The dialogue in the script might as well have been nonexistent. As Jerry, Sally, and Pam look at the wall, Jerry is supposed to say, "What is this? A two-headed zebra?" Sally answers, "No, no, you just can't see his front legs." Pam adds, "It *is* a two-headed zebra!" Then Jerry looks around the room and says, "Who was your decorator? Sargent Shriver?" Not inspired stuff. No wonder they decided to ad-lib.

"Allen—Jerry—and I were up there goofing around in character," Marilyn says. "I looked at the wall and I'm just saying, 'Gosh, I've always had this fascination with the zebras.' Allen Danziger says something like, 'You did? Why?' I looked at him like *Don't screw with me*, because I was so surprised he was going to improvise with me."

"A lot of the lines were changed as we did things," Teri McMinn says. "They would change a scene in a second, and so they would say, 'Well, just say this,' and so I'd just say that."

"Some of it I like, and some of it makes me cringe," Bill Vail says.

Part of the reason that some of this dialogue and character interaction was "not that great," as Teri puts it, might be that the young people in the van were not the characters that Tobe and Kim were focused on. "The fodder characters," Wayne calls them. "You don't really care that much about them. The truth is, the actors' acting, doing lines that were written for them, was the least inspired part of the film and of the film directing. The same was true with *Eggshells*, too, by the way. The straight people acting like people wasn't really Tobe's interest. But when you got to the crazies and doing crazy things, that's where Tobe was very clear about what he wanted. And that was the fun part." It would explain why most of the script rewrites were in the first half of the movie, before the chain saw family takes center stage.

Of course, on-screen the dialogue seems much better, thanks to Tobe's judicious editing and the understanding that often it was needed only to set up a scene. More than that, the dialogue quickly becomes secondary to the scenes themselves and the way they are shot—an occasional long shot that implies the travelers are being watched, the darkness of the house, and even Kirk's discovery of the daddy longlegs and their overlaid wet, slapping sound create a sense of foreboding that can simply overtake the dialogue.

Looking at the movie now, Bill cringes most at his scene with Teri at the dried-out swimming hole. "That's the part I just hate of my improvisation. I just don't like it," he says. "I wish it was better than it was. But you know, in a one-take-and-move-on kind of a situation, it was just like Tobe said, 'Go do this,' and we went 'Oh, okay.'"

He also wishes that their characters had been more sexual toward each other, and so more believable. "In the lead-up to the house, there could have been pats on the butt, there could have been kisses, there could have been hand-holding," he says. "There could have been more little pieces that could have helped in just cementing that relationship a little bit more. I thought we could have been a little more like hot young people instead of an old married couple. It would have made sense. We were finally getting away, if we're going to the swimming hole. It was that 'We're going to take our clothes off and jump in the swimming hole and go have a grand old time.'"

Teri agrees. "I think it would have been more powerful, to be honest with you," she says. "I thought that what they did was not that great, and I think that if they'd had a little more romance, a kiss, just a kiss, I think it would have made their deaths so much more powerful."

However, as Allen says, "This was not an actor's movie. We were there to fill the time till we died."

Maybe that was why Franklin was more interesting than the other "fodder characters." Unlike them, he was at least off balance, if not outright crazy. Unfortunately, Paul behaved just like Franklin his whole time on set, whining and complaining and even staying in his wheelchair when off-camera. The other actors and the crew pretty much thought he was a miserable person, and I, too, quickly grew to dislike him intensely. Maybe, I thought, he was not acting at all.

"Paul was like somebody you played off of, you know what I mean?" Allen says. "His character was hard to like."

"I just thought, 'Why'd they cast this guy?'" Teri says. "I just couldn't figure it out, because he was just a pain in the ass. It was pretty strange dealing with him, and the way I dealt with him in the picture it was sort of like, 'Do we have to bring him along?' Which worked out really well for the character. I know all I kept thinking as Pam was *If we could just get away to some swimming hole.*"

A story has floated around that one day while the actors waited for a shot to be set up, Paul turned to Bill and whined, "Kirk, would you get me a Dr Pepper?" Paul always called the other actors by their character names. Bill pointed at the cooler only feet away and said, "Paul, your legs work just fine. Get up and get it yourself." "Oh. Yeah," Paul said, as if surprised by the fact. He got up and got his Dr Pepper himself. Bill says the story is true.

"He was so obnoxious all the time, and you just knew you didn't want to be with him," Bill recalls. "You wanted to leave him alone, you wanted to leave him in the van and go, 'Fucking figure it out yourself! Get out by yourself!'"

Of course, it was all an act.

Tobe and Wayne filmed Paul in the van while at the gas station. It is a simple scene: Franklin digs his knife into the side of the van, then speculates to Kirk what it must take to cut oneself the way the Hitchhiker did. "Paul really gave it some business, really gave us some interesting stuff happening on his face without having to say much," Wayne says. "There was a real appreciation on our part of when there was good acting, and Paul did deliver it. So the Franklin character, who is a whiny, dislikable character, to make that character so dislikable, that was a real performance on Paul's part."

I never realized it was an act till many years later, when I met up with Paul at a little café in Austin for a cup of coffee. I had not seen him since I had killed him on set. He turned out not to be Franklin at all. For many years after that, whenever I was in town, we would get together for dinner. He confessed to me that he had been scared of "losing" Franklin during the filming and not being able to go into character when Tobe called "Action!" So every day, when he arrived on set, he *became* Franklin. And he stayed Franklin till he left. That was why he stayed in the wheelchair and why he called everyone by his or her character name. His grandfather, he said later, had been in a wheelchair for seven years, and he had watched the man struggle. That is where Franklin came from.

Paul's decision to Method Act, to immerse himself in his character, certainly made for a bit of tension, and a pretty isolated on-set life for Paul. Nobody wanted to be near him. "Yeah, I got a sense that nobody liked Paul Partain," says John, who would not take on the role of Grandpa for weeks but was on set running errands for Tobe ("You know, I'm in the mood for a Snappy Tom! John, would you run up to the UtoteM and get me a Snappy Tom?"). "I got a sense that Paul was kind of lonely. He was the first person that I met the first day that I was there, and he had that '67 Cadillac convertible with the huge fins on it, white with red leather interior. It was so Paul, that car. And he was sitting, I guess, in his wheelchair, and he had a couple of folding chairs out by the rear of his car. The trunk was open, and he had a huge cooler with cold beer in it. He was so starved for just conversation. He said, 'C'mon, have a seat here, partner. Grab yourself a beer.'"

———————

A few days into the filming, something went wrong and filming stopped. This was before I even started work. Memories differ as to exactly what happened—equipment malfunction, money problems, an unhappy producer, an overwhelmed production that needed to catch its breath—each seems plausible among the adventures of independent filmmaking.

I was told at the time that there was a camera problem: The footage (called dailies or rushes) of the first few days of filming had come back from the lab and was unusable. There would be a delay, and then the shooting would have to start over. Tobe has confirmed this, saying in an interview that a 10-mm lens "went bad." Cinematographer Daniel Pearl and production manager Ron Bozman also cite a lens problem.

Editor Larry Carroll thinks that it had come down to money, that Tobe had run out and that executive producer Jay Parsley was "very worried about his investment." To Larry's way of thinking, the "camera problem might have been a convenient cover for the financial problem."

Wayne, though, believes it was something other than money. "I suspect it was about seeing this kind of improv stuff done at the abandoned house," he says. "Seeing that it was kind of boring."

From Marilyn's perspective, both might be right. "Parsley looked at the early footage, and we got hell for how bad we were. And then the guys that put the money up saw footage, and they were unhappy. They came to me and they said, 'How did you let this happen?' But I think, considering where the film's been and why we're talking about it forty years later, they might have been wrong about that first week."

I recall that at some point the producers did raise more money. The film was originally scheduled for three weeks of production. It stretched to six. My original two weeks expanded to four. Tobe could not have extended the shooting schedule without more money. And money was a constant topic on set.

Kim Henkel's take differs. "Really the issue—and I'm going on memory here—is that we were just not properly organized and we were missing too many elements. Tobe got out on the set with certain expectations of things being in place and they weren't there. So we needed to regroup and make sure the things that we needed when we walked out on the set to shoot it would be in place."

According to Daniel, it was during this time Ron insisted that Tobe develop a shot list for each day's shooting. This would speed the production along. Ron agrees that he likely did require a shot list at that point. "You know there was nervousness just about Tobe's work and habits and just a certain free-form about how things were put together," he says.

"Nobody could figure out what Tobe was doing, I think to some degree even Tobe," Larry says. "It was certainly not conventional filmmaking or, I should say, conventional low-budget filmmaking. Big-budget film you can reshoot something or suddenly see the opportunity to do something, but on a low-budget film, that's just unheard of. You have a shot list, you know what scenes you're going to get out of the way. The director's got his number of setups planned well in advance so everybody knows what's going on. There's not a whole lot of wiggle room."

"On the first day of our being back," Daniel says, "I showed up at the set and proceeded to try to make the setup for shot number one on the shot list. Tobe showed up sometime like fifteen, twenty minutes later, and came in and just undid everything that I had gotten going, changed it all. Okay, I went along with that, he's the director, and I assume that part of your job is to realize the director's vision.

"Well, the next day, a similar thing happened. I showed up and started working, getting the setup made as it was described in the shot list for that day, and Tobe, again, when he showed up, changed everything. At that point I said, 'Tobe, what's going on here, man?' 'Oh,' he said, 'didn't I tell you? They made me write that shot list. I just wrote that to get them to shut up. We're not doing that. It's something I just dashed out.' I said, 'Well, okay, I'm glad I know that now.'"

"I think it quickly revealed itself," Ron says of the shot list, that "it was not in the DNA of the movie, and you just had to go with it. You just had to go with Tobe's way of shooting, and you couldn't really change it or fight it because it was his way of doing it, and that's what ended up being the creative engine of the film—and the brilliance of the film."

CHAPTER 5

YOU BOYS DON'T WANT TO GO MESSIN' AROUND IN SOME OLD HOUSE

My first day of filming finally arrived. This would not be some Mexican romance walk-through. Leatherface was going to kill Kirk. With a sledgehammer. And Kirk was going to die well. I would make sure of that.

But first I had to deal with the reality of the wardrobe. The clothes themselves were simple enough—blue dress pants, my shirt, a goofy blue tie with a scalloped silver curve painted on it, and a yellow butcher's apron. But my old cowboy boots had now been fitted with new soles and three-inch heels, transforming me from a bulky six-foot-four to a hulking six-foot-seven. I knew this would make me look more imposing on-screen, but it also likely could cause some problems for me while running through the woods at night or even sooner. I was right, and it would be worse than I feared.

Then there were the masks—the three different faces that Leatherface wears at different times—each full-head covering including hair, as if the victims' entire heads had been skinned. We called the first the "Killing Mask," described in the script as "a close fitting hood rather than a mask, covering the entire head and slit to accommodate the ears. The face of the hood is human but shriveled and leathery." Leatherface wears this from his first appearance till the end of chasing Sally through the woods. The second is described as "the tanned facial skin of an elderly woman; it has been stretched over a rigid form to give it the proper shape." This I always thought of as the "Old Lady." Its hair is gray, pulled up in a bun. Leatherface wears it only briefly, when the Cook and the Hitchhiker bring Sally home. On set we called the third mask the "Pretty Woman." It is "the face of a woman who might once have been beautiful. The process of tanning the flesh has shrunken the size of the features and given them a deep mahogany tint. The mask has been made up with a white powder and has some of the starkness of stage makeup. The lips are heavily ringed with a dark red lipstick, the eyebrows penciled in darkly with mascara, the lashes have been covered with false ones and around the eyes there is a greenish eye shadow." Its hair is long and black, with a loose curl. Kim Henkel calls it the "Clarabell Clown" mask. Leatherface wears this from the dinner scene till the end.

Each of these masks represents something to—and within— Leatherface. Early on, Tobe told me that Leatherface wears different faces because he is showing who he is right then. He uses the masks to express the context he is in and how he will behave—his state of mind. When the Hitchhiker and the Cook bring Sally to the house, Leatherface, in his Old Lady mask, is making dinner and being "mom" for a while. He later puts on the Pretty Woman face to dress up for dinner. In a way the masks are theatrical for Leatherface. They are performance.

And as the shooting wore on, the significance of the masks to Leatherface would become more important for me in the way I played him. Leatherface is an enigmatic character. Behind the mask he is, in essence, unknown and unknowable. I began to feel that each mask did not merely represent how he felt; it *was* how he felt. Everything was in the mask, and beneath it there really was nothing at all. Eventually this extended to my thinking of

Leatherface as having no face at all. Take off his mask and you find nothing—featureless skin or even nothingness itself. Leatherface is empty.

Bob Burns designed and constructed all three masks, working from face molds created by plastic surgeon Dr. William Barnes, a friend of Marilyn Burns. "We got a bunch of people to volunteer to [sit for the molds]," Kim says, "and some of them found the process unbearable and said, 'Get me out of here! I can't handle this.' Others survived it, and we had a number of death masks cast. I don't remember who-all we did it to."

One of the mask-model volunteers was executive producer Jay "Bill" Parsley. The mask made from his face worked very well. "It did look like Bill Parsley, and that was so funny," Marilyn says. "Both Dr. Barnes and Bill Parsley were so proud of doing that cast on his face. They were really going to screw up the producer's mask so it really looked bad as Leatherface." This became the Killing Mask.

Mary Church says Bob "spent weeks trying to come up with just homemade varieties of stuff that sort of looked like dried skin. I remember him being concerned about expression, or not being able to do expression, and that there probably needed to be other expressions maybe on the face."

Bob once said that, after quite a bit of experimentation, he finally figured out the right materials to make the mask—liquid latex and thin insulation. It aged naturally, turning a brownish yellow.

The masks had one unfortunate feature—their eyeholes were small. They fit snugly, but not around my eyes, and the further the eyeholes were from my face, the less I could see. It was like looking down a long tube—I could see only what was directly in front of me. I figured this might also become a problem. And again it would prove worse than I feared.

There was one other bit of makeup for Leatherface, his teeth. In the script they are mentioned only once. When the Cook and the Hitchhiker arrive with Sally, "There is a flash of filed teeth."

One curious thing about the teeth: They were made by different dentists, depending on whom you talk to. Daniel Pearl says that before the shooting even started, his wife, Dottie, had had them made. On the other hand, Larry Carroll says his father-in-law, a dentist in San Antonio, made them. Both stories are wrong. The teeth were made by my dentist, Dr. Albert Johnson, who had a practice on 15th and Lavaca Streets in Austin. I remember clearly that Dr. Johnson said making them would be straightforward because he already had a full-mouth impression of me from some earlier work—and I clearly remember the misery of that process.

I also remember that I was disappointed when I saw them. I had expected to see fangs—adult teeth, each one filed to a single point—and instead the dentist used baby teeth. They were irregular, and each was filed to two points. The effect was a saw-edged smile. Of course, those baby teeth proved far more frightening than what I had been imagining, and they raised another question about Leatherface himself—why did this hulking creature still have baby teeth?

Once I was in costume, Tobe told me to stay away from the other actors. They wanted to feel genuinely frightened when they first faced me on camera, he said. It would be all the more realistic.

As little as I knew about acting, I knew that this was not what it was about, at least to me. The actor's job was to create an illusion, not the real thing. It just needed to look or feel like the real thing—in this case, fear—*to the audience*. Leatherface's victims needed to look fearful, but they did not necessarily need to be fearful. Often the real fear could get in the way.

I certainly did not want to be Leatherface, or even feel his emotions. For me he was a shell, a set of behaviors and postures. I was so separate from him that when I looked in the mirror in makeup, I was looking at Leatherface, not myself as Leatherface. This was another person, and I did not see myself in him at all. Maybe this is why, in spite of what I am often asked, I never suffered nightmares from playing the character.

Even the few times I had worked on stage, where I might have made use of such character immersion, some inner part of me had always sat back and watched, managing what was happening on my outside. When I played Lennie in *Of Mice and Men*, even though he was crying after killing the puppy, inside I certainly was not. In fact, I was surprised when Lennie started crying. I heard audience members starting to sniffle and I remember thinking that I had them where I wanted them.

This separation was what had allowed the outside part of me to act out safely. If Leatherface had been part of me, the psychological burden would have been overwhelming. I really would have ended up becoming that mythical, permanently damaged, poetic soul.

Did the other actors not feel the same way?

"I heard [from Tobe] that we would be more frightened if we met you as Leatherface and we didn't get too chummy as friends," Marilyn says. "We might have heard you were a loner, too. You know, 'Besides, he's a loner anyway, so it doesn't matter.' He was manipulating an actor before he even had to manipulate him."

"I remember him wanting to keep us separate," Bill Vail says. "We didn't, like, 'Let's go have lunch. Let's go shoot a game of pool. Let's go hang out and drink a beer.' One day after we shot, we went and sat on the back porch and smoked marijuana with Tobe and me and a couple other people. But I don't remember you being there; I don't remember Ed being there. There were two families and he wanted to keep us separate."

"Yeah, I always thought that was stupid," Ed Neal says, "because I can be me, I can be Ed Neal until the fucking camera rolls, and then when the camera rolls, then I'll be that other guy. I always thought that was silly. You sitting over there by yourself and people walking around you. I went, *What the hell? What was that all about?*"

Not that other directors weren't above such tricks to create a kind of real emotion in their actors. In *The Birds* (1963), director Alfred Hitchcock famously pulled one on Tippi Hedren. He assured her that in the scene where she would encounter an attic full of birds, the creatures would be mechanical. Of course, just before they shot the scene, a crew member came to her room to tell her that the mechanical birds were not working and they would have to use live ones. He would not look at her when he said it. And, she adds, she knew then that they never intended to use mechanical birds—all this in the hope of having her show "genuine" fear and panic in front of the camera.

Curiously, this bit of trickery was just about all the direction we actors got from Tobe. His genius lay elsewhere. Or maybe his genius also lay in otherwise leaving us alone.

"He was so consumed by the minutiae of moving lights and camera and physical things that there wasn't a lot of discussion," Ed says of Tobe's instructions to him. "In fact, pretty much the entire directorial advice boiled down into one sentence. He goes, 'Well, do some more of that Strother Martin stuff.' [Martin was the actor who played the prison warden in *Cool Hand Luke*.] And that was pretty much it. That was pretty much all he ever told me."

Almost all the direction I got from Tobe was blocking—where he wanted me to move through the scene. Actually, I was glad that his directing was so minimal. I was pretty much able to find and create Leatherface, myself, and play him the way I wanted.

Ed agrees. "Every actor wants to think that they can create something on their own rather than being force-fed," he says. "A lot of young directors will give line readings and tell you exactly what to do, and they go overboard. So you're always fearful of that, but, luckily for us, there was none of that."

———•———

Kirk is about to become dead meat, with Pam soon to follow. At the dried up swimming hole, they hear the generator running at the chain saw family house and walk over to see if they can borrow gas. As they do, they pass a shredded camp—a torn up tent with some debris hanging from a shrub like a grotesque Christmas tree. The view is a long one, as if something near the shrub is watching as they pass in the background. Then in close-up we see hanging from it a pocket watch with a spike through it. It's an interesting shot, a bit of Salvador Dalí inserted into an entirely unexpected context, an oblique reference to his 1931 painting *The Persistence of Memory*, in which time has stopped. (*Chain Saw* also shares elements with Dalí's 1929 short *Un Chien Andalou*. Aside from their surrealism, both create brutal illusions—a razor slicing through woman's eye in *Un Chien*, the chain saw slicing Franklin in half in *Chain Saw*. In fact, critic Jonathan Rosenbaum noted in his 1983 book *Midnight Movies* that he'd noticed London's Whiskey-A-Go-Go featuring a film program of *Un Chien Andalou* screening with excerpts from *Chain Saw*.) Also, Franklin's earlier encounter with the bone-and-feather "nest" and the hanging bone fetish already hints that someone in the chain saw family has a bit of *artistic* interest. This spiked watch is maybe the next hint.

Of course Kirk and Pam don't notice any of this. They get to the house, where Kirk teases her with a human molar that he has picked up on the porch. Pam stalks off in irritation to the swing set, and Kirk then goes inside. The price of this trespassing is a short, blunt chat with Leatherface.

———◆———

I was scared to death. This would be my first time on camera, and I wanted it to be perfect. Oh, was it ever perfect.

The scene was to be very simple: Kirk walks down the hall and trips on the ramp leading to the "bone room," the small room with the skulls on the wall. (It had a raised floor meant to simulate the slatted floor at a slaughterhouse.) Leatherface steps out and whacks him with the sledge. Kirk falls and Leatherface drags his body out of the doorway. Then he slides the metal door shut.

Bill thought the scene as written lacked something. "I have always been a very physical actor," he says. "I enjoy that part. I just went, *It needs to be more than that*. Also I remember the quote from, I think it was Jimmy Cagney, 'No good actor dies quickly.' I thought, *This is my big moment. I'm gone from the movie after this, and I want it to be more. It's the first death of the movie. It's got to be more than just boom, boom, done."*

So Bill summoned his courage and suggested some changes to Tobe, including having Leatherface's blow spin Kirk's head, with his body following. "And Tobe got off on it," Bill says. "'And then you spasm, and then you spit out the blood, and then you do this, and then you do this.' 'And then I can do this.' And then we were feeding off of each other. So that's kind of how it evolved. I think it was very effective, and works for the movie, and was a good beginning."

And it was. But it turned out to be a bit more real than Bill had expected.

I would, of course, be using a fake sledgehammer, even though my blow was to miss Bill. Propmaster Bob Burns had made it with a foam rubber head, but it looked just like our real one. I was to sweep the sledge past Bill's head so that to the camera it would look like I hit him. And then he would execute his midair flip and land on his back. I would deliver the fake *coup de grâce* and drag him out of the way. The crew had accommodated Bill by laying pillows on the floor so I could drop him on them. All very quick, smooth, and painless.

Unfortunately, it did not quite work that way. I was nervous. And I was completely charged up on adrenaline, skittishly hopping back and forth as if I were speeding. So when Bill tripped and I stepped out of the shadows, I actually hit him in the face with the sledgehammer. Fake or not, it left its mark.

"The first time you really hit me, you hauled off and whacked me and broke some blood vessels," Bill says. "Then we did it again and you lightened up on the second and third times. But that first time you really hit me, and even though it was foam, I felt it. It stung."

Bill, on the other hand, did his job perfectly. I was amazed to see his flip—he rotated his head when I hit him, and at the same time his feet came off the floor. Then his entire body rolled in midair to follow his head so that he landed on his back. He began to spasm, which I believe made the scene work. I was so impressed watching him at the time, in fact, that I wonder now how I even remembered what to do next.

I finished him off—not a direct blow this time—and picked him up to drag him out of the way. Except that I did not drag him out of the way. In my excitement, I tossed him. He flew headlong into the wall, well off the floor. The pillows did cushion his landing when he finally came to rest.

I was concentrating on my next task, closing the sliding metal door, and had no idea that I had just knocked Bill silly. I was supposed to just slide it shut and be done with it. But my heart was racing, and I was so excited that I did not realize how much force I was using. As I started to pull the door closed, I left my feet, hopping forward to give myself more leverage. I slammed the door as if it weighed nothing. And because of its construction, when the door hit the frame, it jammed, stopping dead, as if I had just flipped a half-ton door closed.

"Ron Bozman, I never saw this guy move so fast," Bill says. "But after you threw me into the wall, he came running back there. 'Are you okay? Are you okay?' He just saw the whole movie coming to an end because I had been crippled and I was going to sue, and I've broken my neck, or something horrible for his movie. He was very upset."

Poor Bill was semiconscious. But on-screen the whole thing looks great. In fact, it looks perfect. And Bill, all these years later, says it's his favorite scene in *Chain Saw*. "I just like it," he says. "I feel like I nailed the death scene."

Doug Bradley, "Pinhead" of the *Hellraiser* movies, has an interesting perspective on the scene. "If you are making a Dracula movie," he says, "when Dracula makes his first appearance in the doorway, you're going to have the big hero close-up, Dracula in the doorway. *Your* first appearance, you're in and out. We barely get a chance to register—who is it? Is he wearing a mask? I was intrigued watching it as an actor, because I know that, honestly, my feeling at the time would have been 'Where's the coverage? Why didn't I get a close-up?' It wouldn't have been until I saw the film that I would have thought that's the thing to have done."

This is an essential quality in *The Texas Chain Saw Massacre*: these events are casual; they seem to happen in real time. The movie, as Marilyn says, "keeps going like real life does." There is no lingering on the image, making sure the audience sees *exactly* what just happened or what is about to happen. That casualness is part of *Chain Saw*'s seeming realism and, at this point in the movie, it keeps Leatherface a mystery to the audience. What have they just seen? What they *imagine* they have seen is much richer than what they would actually have seen had he gotten his close-up.

CHAPTER 6

IF I HAVE ANY MORE FUN I DON'T THINK I CAN TAKE IT

I suppose I should tell you about the marijuana crop. It will explain Bill Vail's earlier reference to sitting on the porch smoking, as well as some later goings-on. Memory being what it is, especially after a few tokes, there are two different, though closely related, versions of the story. I will tell both.

Daniel Pearl says that a day or two after we started shooting at the chain saw family house, the man who actually lived there—he had moved out for the duration—came up to him. "He goes, 'You seem to be somebody who might know what's going on around here,'" Daniel says. "'They told me you guys were coming up for three days, but you've pretty well moved in here. It doesn't look like you are out of here any time soon.' And I said, 'Three days? We're probably here for three weeks.' He goes, 'Oh my God! Three weeks. I guess I'd better tell you what's going on. I've got two acres of marijuana growing out back. So I'm telling you guys now, you can feel free to pick and dry whatever you might want for your personal consumption, but please don't take anything off the property.'"

I wish *I* had known about this. I even had the guy's phone number written on my script, between Kim Henkel's and Ron Bozman's. I must have been blind, because I never noticed the crop though I spent much of my time between scene setups out in the back field running—I was worried about lasting through the chase scenes and wanted to be ready.

Ron has a slightly different—and scarier—account. "When we were putting the film together I went to see the sheriff of Williamson County," he says. "Tough, crusty old son of a bitch." This was Sheriff Jim Boutwell, already famous for his heroics during Charlie Whitman's 1966 sniper attack from the University of Texas tower, in which Whitman killed thirteen people. Boutwell had commandeered an airplane and circled the tower while a police sharpshooter aboard fired at Whitman. That lasted till Whitman started shooting back.

"In his waiting room there's a whole little exhibit of drug paraphernalia and stuff," Ron continues. "He was just this big, tall, lanky guy. I said, 'We're going to be making this movie. Just wanted you to know. Anybody calls, you know what's going on out there. Just come by and see us anytime.' Then one day I was walking through the house and went to the back porch, which is screened in. I looked up, and it was packed with eight-foot high marijuana plants, just packed with weed. I said, 'Oh, my God.' As I walked back to the house, I said, 'Kim, we're in deep shit here.' Then Parsley drove up and I thought, *Oh fuck! What do I do?* Parsley was vice president of Texas Tech. He'd been in the legislature. He was a prominent character in the state of Texas. So I took him back there. I said, 'Parsley, let me show you something.' We both walked to the back. He looked at it and said, 'Oh, what are these? Sunflowers or something?' I said, 'It's marijuana.' He turned white as a ghost, and he said, 'I think I better leave.' He got in his car and drove away.

"I thought, *I'm going to jail,*" Ron says. "I mean, it was really like, the sheriff is going to show up today, you know. I made it very clear to him. 'Come on by!' I thought, *We're in such trouble*. Kim called the guy and said, 'You got to get this stuff out of here.' They would have shut the movie down. Someone would have gone to jail."

At this time in Texas, possession of *any* amount of marijuana was a felony, with sentences ranging from two years to life.

Ron adds, "I think some of our crew quietly poached a little bit of it." No surprise there. In both accounts clearly some crew and actors found the supply conveniently near at hand.

I'm not sure I know exactly who did what or who smoked with whom, but Daniel does tell a little anecdote that might apply. Early one day he was setting up an interior scene. Tobe arrived. "He goes, 'Oh, Daniel, does it have to be so bright in here?'" Daniel says, "In the meantime we *were* shooting a movie."

"Yeah," John Dugan says, "there was a rule that we weren't supposed to smoke on the set, but . . ." He laughs. And so the seed of one of the myths about *The Texas Chain Saw Massacre* was sown. We would forever be thought of as a bunch of stoners out to have some twisted fun.

———•———

Kirk is dead. And now the audience knows that Pam will die next. The sound gives it away. When Leatherface slams the metal door after hammering Kirk, we hear an ominous tone, an extension of the door's slam, only much lower pitched. That tone seems to pull us down with it. And as it fades out slowly, it carries over into the next shot, Pam outside on the swing. That tone hooks Pam's scene to the previous one and tells us that the bad stuff is just not over and the planets are, indeed, badly aligned for these two. (A quick aside: according to Bob Burns, the swing was built for Leatherface. He was a big kid, so he needed a big swing, built with railroad ties.)

It's a great scene, and more sophisticated than it might seem at first. When Pam gets no response from Kirk, she stands up and walks toward the house. We follow under the swing, gliding low to the ground. As she approaches, the house begins to loom over her, as if it is about to swallow her. In a way it does.

There's a certain pleasure in watching Teri McMinn's Pam walk to the house, though it is one of the few such moments in the movie. As boom operator Wayne Bell explains, "Teri had just this little skimpy outfit that you can't help but watch."

At first, Teri did not want to do the shot, her objection very straightforward: the camera would follow right behind her, staring up at her backside as she walked along in this "skimpy outfit." To make it worse, she was told about the shot only as the crew was setting it up. She felt "sabotaged."

"It wasn't brought up to me like, 'Teri, we're going to do a shot and it's going to be, you'll see, it's going to be a great shot. I don't want you to feel uncomfortable.' They snuck it right on me. I didn't respect that."

Despite her discomfort, Teri relented and now agrees that it is one of the best shots in the movie.

In fact, no one was trying to sneak anything past her. Daniel had thought of this shot only the night before. In the script the stage directions for Pam say simply, "She pauses for a moment then stands, a bit peeved, and walks to the steps." It remained to be seen how he and Tobe would pull it off.

"The swing scene is one of the most graphic memories I have of filming," Daniel says. They had just finished shooting Pam sitting on the swing when he turned to Tobe to explain the shot. To get it, he would have to lay track under the swing and lie on a low platform dolly, holding the camera as low as possible off its front. He would keep the track just out of the shot, and the wide-angle lens would distort the house above Teri. And, as Daniel said to Tobe, "The house will grow and grow and grow and envelop the frame." The whole while, Teri would be the center of attention.

"Tobe goes 'Oh damn, man, what a great idea,'" Daniel says. "'Go ahead and set it up.' So we start setting up to make that shot. Production goes, 'So what are you guys doing?' And we explained the shot. They go, 'No, no, no, it's not on the shot list. You guys have to adhere to the shot list. We are not going to let you shoot that shot.' And Tobe goes, 'You know what, you can't stop us. I'm the director, he's the cinematographer. We're going to shoot this shot.'"

As Tobe once said in a *Chain Saw* commentary, "They threatened to fire us if we shot. We threatened to quit if we didn't."

Production manager Ron Bozman is the one who likely was doing the objecting, since his job was to keep everything moving efficiently. "I think the general concept was trying to impose discipline on the shooting, some classic discipline," he says. "And there was a certain amount of conflict. But I think at a certain point that faded away. In hindsight it was a losing battle and, ultimately, not one worth winning. Some of those shots really had made the film just visually stunning."

So they shot it Daniel's way. The camera rolled, and the grips pushed the dolly forward. As soon as Teri was off the swing, two crew members stepped forward and lifted it by its chains so it flew out of the shot as the camera rolled under it. The camera moved smoothly right behind Teri. I remember that we had very little dolly track, so to get a long enough roll on the dolly, some grips had to disconnect the track section Daniel had already rolled over and carry it forward in the middle of the take and reattach it to the front of the track—all without being seen on camera. (Marilyn also remembers this; Daniel does not.)

"That is regarded by a lot of people as one of the greatest dolly shots of all time, most poignant dolly shots of film history," Daniel says. "They say the dolly was [perfected] by F. W. Murnau, was put to great use by Alfred Hitchcock, and was taken even one step further by Jean-Luc Godard, but the greatest dolly shot of all time is Daniel Pearl's shot in *Texas Chain Saw Massacre*."

It has certainly been noticed. Ed Neal says he was cast in Oliver Stone's *JFK* (1991) because of *Chain Saw* and that shot.

Stone "would be asking me questions whenever he could," Ed says, "like 'How'd they do that thing where the camera goes underneath the swing and then the swing disappears?' Then I told him it was just lifted up by some crew members. He goes, 'That can't be true.' I said, 'Oh, but it is.' He was trying to imagine how they flew the swing set out with giant dollies and cranes and all this crap. I said, 'No, you dig up a bunch of crew members who are very strong, and they just lift it up.'"

Daniel has a similar story. "I was introduced to Steven Spielberg when he was shooting *1941*," he says. Dottie, Daniel's wife and *Chain Saw*'s makeup artist, was doing makeup on the movie, so he got onto the otherwise closed set. "When they introduced me they said, 'Steven, this is Daniel Pearl.' He said, 'Daniel Pearl, Daniel Pearl. You shot *The Texas Chain Saw Massacre*.' Puts his arm around me and says, 'That shot on the swing, you know, tell me about that.' And he proceeds to walk me off the set, leaves his crew of about eighty or a hundred standing there, and takes me to John Belushi's trailer. John Belushi's in the trailer dressed up; he's got his wardrobe on for the movie. Spielberg's sitting there in front of me about three feet, four feet away from me, basically vacuuming my brain on everything he wanted to know about *Texas Chain Saw Massacre*. I'm totally astounded. This is insane. Here I am with Spielberg in my face and Belushi behind him doing shtick. It was very, very surreal."

Now Pam enters the house. I guess she has no fear invading a private home, either. Look where it got Kirk. Things will quickly get nasty for her. And for poor old Leatherface, for that matter.

She walks into the dimly lit dining room, and then into the living room, giving the audience its first chance to really see the interior. We have already glimpsed a bit when Kirk dies, a brief view of the animal skulls mounted on the red wall in that little room behind the metal door, but this is our first good look at Bob's set design in its full, carnivorous glory. Feathers and teeth and dissected electronics litter the floor. Various artifacts, including a skeletal hand, a small animal's rib cage, and a human skull with a horn rammed through its mouth, hang from the ceiling. Skulls, jawbones, and leg bones fill a wire basket. Cowhides cover much of the walls. A bone couch and bone chairs populate the room. None of them looks very comfortable. A human spine hangs nearby.

Aside from being gruesome, the set also stank. In that heat, the bones and hides and animal parts were letting off a rich mix of fumes. Add the sweating humans and the lack of ventilation, and it quickly got ripe inside. It certainly enriched the atmosphere of the shoot.

"It gave you the creeps," says Stuart Gordon. "When you're watching the movie, you can almost smell that smell. You just feel the sense of you're in a bad place, this is not going to come out well. [Bob] doesn't do things traditionally at all, and as a result he can really capture stuff that you don't see in other movies."

Bill Vail, who has worked many years now as a Hollywood set decorator himself, views Bob's design as "another character in the movie. The movie would not have been the same without it."

The contents of the room return us to an earlier question. Aren't these objects some sort of art, as with the spiked clock and the nest and hanging bone fetish found by Franklin, intentionally constructed to have some meaning to their makers? They also recall the "macabre necrophiliac art," as Wayne Bell called it, of the gooey body and skull impaled on the graveyard obelisk at the beginning of the film as the radio announcer talks of grave desecration, the implication being that these are the work of the Hitchhiker and Leatherface. Is one of them some kind of artist? If so, what does that mean about his mentality?

There was also a live chicken in the living room, filling a small birdcage that dangled from the ceiling. That chicken caused some worry for Bob. "That was funny about the chicken," editor Larry Carroll says. "I knew there was a live chicken in that room and I went to the set one day and I remember Robert Burns, God rest his soul, he was just livid because he was convinced that Tobe was going to do something to that chicken, and he was saying, 'If he does, I'm taking all my props and everything and I'm leaving!'"

Bob had reason to worry for that chicken's safety, but that was because of the heat. "I would be going down to the slaughterhouse at the end of Red River," Kim says. Red River Street, in Austin, ran south to the Colorado River. "Right down on the banks of the river there was a chicken slaughterhouse during that time. I'd go down there about five in the morning. Chickens escaped, and there was this pen out in the back of the slaughterhouse where the escaped chickens got to. So they would sell me a chicken for fifty cents. Well, I had to go out there and chase it down. So I was out there like Rocky Balboa at five in the morning trying to chase a goddamned chicken down to put in a cage, because they were always dying." Apparently Bob did not know that they were dying and being replaced, since he never removed his props.

And in the middle of this heat, Pam comes stumbling into this bizarre room. Literally. In the script, she "stumbles through the curtains, trips, tears the curtains from their rod and crashes to the floor in a heap of bones." Teri asked Tobe why Pam would trip, and they put a bucket in her way.

"It was one of those old galvanized buckets, and it had a sharp edge on it," she says. "They couldn't figure out to just line the bucket with some sponge or something to keep it from cutting. It recut my leg every time. I remember the exact point on my shin where it would hit. I remember because it was just so painful. I mean I'm sure I tried to not kick it the same way, but I had open-toed shoes on so I didn't have a lot of options. If I did it right the next time, I kept thinking, we won't have to shoot it again. Well, wrong."

Teri, and Pam, survived it. But not for long, at least for Pam. She gags—I have wondered if it is from the feathers floating in the air—and panics. As she tries to make a fast exit, Leatherface comes out from behind his sliding door, lets out a howl—yes, *that* howl—and chases her down the hall. He catches her on the front porch, wrapping his arms around her waist and lifting her off her feet as she thrashes uselessly, and then hauling her back inside. So far this was going all right for me. I could see just enough to run down the hall safely, though the raised heels on my boots made me a bit unsteady.

"The first forty-five times it wasn't as painful as the last," Teri says, exaggerating a bit. "We took it all so seriously. We wanted these scenes to look really good, so I was screaming and flailing and fighting. I did it all day. Well, as tired as you got with me doing that, I was tired, too, because you were really strong and I couldn't get out of the lock. I was so exhausted, and my voice, at about five or six o'clock, was gone. I was hoarse and [Tobe] still wanted to do other angles, other shots. And so I said, 'Tobe, I can't scream.'" So, for the last hour of filming they started giving her shots of Jack Daniel's between takes. She says it did relax her. Part of Teri's concern for her throat was that she was appearing on stage that night as the lead in *The Rainmaker* and would be needing her voice.

Once we shot Leatherface's catching Pam on the front porch, we had to move inside for the rest of the sequence, starting with his carrying her down the hall and through the metal door into the bone room. This would present me with problems of my own.

After the lighting and camera were set, we did a slow walk-through before filming to make sure everything worked. To give Teri a rest, Mary Church doubled for her. Everything went fine the first time with Mary. I walked down the hall and through the doorway. Because we were doing it slowly, I did not carry her the way I otherwise would. Instead of standing fully upright, letting my back muscles bear the strain of carrying her as she struggled in my arms, I bent forward to balance her weight and take the load off my back as I walked.

Then we did the real-time run-through, the final rehearsal before we actually filmed. Again I carried Mary. But this time I was running, as I would be during filming, so I stood upright as I came down the hall with Mary struggling in my grasp.

The problem was that I did not clear the doorway. In the boots I was now six-foot-seven. There was a ramp at the doorway to accommodate the little bone room's raised floor. That brought the floor up about four inches, reducing the headroom from six-foot-eight to about six-foot-four. Add the fact that I could barely see out of the mask, and I was about to meet trouble.

Ever wonder what happens when an unstoppable force meets an unmovable object? One of them becomes either stoppable or movable. I became stoppable.

I hit the doorway with a loud crack that rang through my head, as well as the room. I dropped Mary and fell backward, landing stretched out on the floor. I think I lost consciousness for a moment. Mary was worried I'd cracked my skull.

I opened my eyes to see Tobe kneeling beside me, peering into the mask. I vaguely remember that he said something like, "Are you all right?" I nodded. Then he said, "Okay, let's take a break."

I sat up and said no, that I was all right and that we should go ahead with the shot. That was fine with Tobe, and we shot the scene. I do not remember how many takes we did. I do remember that I had a headache for the rest of the day.

We were already so caught up in the filming—*I* was so caught up in the filming—that I did not want to stop. I did not care about the injury. I just wanted to keep going. Maybe the first seeds of madness were now planted, when the film became bigger than us. We certainly would slide into some kind of irrational passion as the filming wore on.

When you watch the scene now, you can see that Leatherface carries Pam down the hall at a leisurely pace. And when he reaches the ramp, he slows even more and bends over, just to make sure he clears the door. It is oh-so-slow. But it looks pretty good.

I just wish we had that original head crack on film.

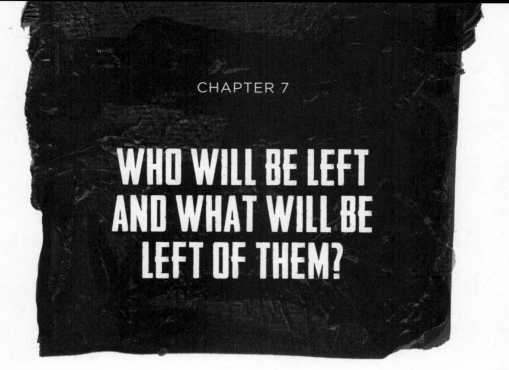

CHAPTER 7

WHO WILL BE LEFT AND WHAT WILL BE LEFT OF THEM?

Bob Burns was worried about the meat hook scene. Hanging Pam had looked pretty straightforward—put Teri McMinn in a harness and then hang the harness on the meat hook. But Bob had not figured on Teri's wardrobe. Her shorts and backless bathing suit were so minimal that he did not know how he would get a harness on her without having it visible. He let everyone, including me, know he was not happy.

"I remember Burns just going ballistic when he saw that outfit on Teri," editor Larry Carroll says. "*How am I going to do this?!* I don't think Teri was happy about being hung up there, because I'm sure she was hung up there for hours. Thank gosh she was a little bitty thing, because it was easy to sort of pick her up and get her down."

Bob eventually came up with a solution, though not a comfortable one for Teri.

"Oh yeah, I remember it specifically," Teri says. "It was like a Kotex belt, or a chastity belt. It had foam in the bottom for the crotch to take the weight."

"You know, we probably went to Army Surplus and got some sort of parachutist sort of thing," Mary Church says, "and then just whittled it and whittled it. I don't remember how Bob carved it all down, but I know it was a process."

Dottie Pearl came up with the idea to hold it all together with panty hose, which she sewed into the "chastity belt" and then carried up around Teri's neck, under her hair, and pinned inside her costume so it could not be seen.

A strap with a ring at its end came up Teri's back from the harness. It would be tucked within her costume when the camera showed her back as I lifted her to the hook. Then, when the camera was looking over my shoulder at her, the strap and ring would be back in place. They were what Teri would hang from. According to Teri, Dottie spent most of the night before shooting the scene sewing this all together.

In the meantime, aside from her harness concerns, Teri had been thinking about how she would do the scene. "I was worried about how I'd play a woman on a meat hook," she says. "I do remember the day we were going to shoot it, Tobe said, 'So, Teri, have you thought about what you're going to do in the scene?' I said, 'Well, Tobe, the only thing I can come up with is if somebody were trying to put me on a meat hook, I would be trying to get off.'" Simple as it sounds, it was convincing—and horrifying—on camera.

I approached the hook carrying Teri still facing away from me, my arms around her as she struggled. Then I dropped her, and she turned to run around me, as if she really thought she could escape. I grabbed her again and carried her the last steps to the hook. But now she was facing me. This breakaway had been Tobe's idea, to get her turned around so her back would face the hook. Though it was actually a bit of business added to resolve a logistical problem, on camera it looks quite natural, and the scene is the better for it. Teri says that this short escape is her favorite moment in what is now her favorite scene.

Once I had Teri in place, I lifted her toward the hook, with the camera filming from behind me. I remember that she seemed to weigh nothing. Then we shot from the opposite direction, with the camera high up in the corner looking down at Teri, the hook dominating the foreground as I lifted her toward it—and with the harness strap tucked away. The next shot was from behind me again. With the camera off, the crew turned the meat hook around to point away from Teri, I lifted her up, and we threaded the harness ring onto the hook. When we rolled the camera, I was already holding her at full height. I dropped her down till the backward-pointing hook caught the ring and stopped her short, as if it had dug into her back. Hanging Pam, as Mary says, "was like hanging a picture."

Those shots cut together smooth and fast, and many people are not aware that they have seen three separate shots. Rather, they are convinced they have just seen the hook penetrate Pam's back. And many remember the scene as filled with gore.

This is the same reaction Quentin Tarantino gets in his 1992 *Reservoir Dogs* in the scene in which Mr. Blonde cuts the cop's ear off. In an interview after the film's release, Tarantino said he first shot the scene showing the ear being sliced. He then did an alternative shot, letting the camera turn discreetly away as Mr. Blonde cuts the ear. This, he said, was insurance in case the explicit shot was too shocking. But when he cut the scene together, the explicit shot was flat. He substituted the less graphic alternative and found it much more disturbing. That is the shot that made it into the movie. Sometimes the unseen is much more powerful than the seen, especially in a movie like *The Texas Chain Saw Massacre*.

Tobe has said that the hook scene is the one that people walked out on in early screenings because of what they thought they were seeing. Even now, forty years later, audiences who see it on the big screen—audiences who know this movie—will laugh and cheer when Leatherface hammers Kirk and then fall silent when Pam goes onto the hook. Though they know what is coming, they are still unnerved by what they see. Or don't see.

To *Hellraiser*'s Doug Bradley, the scene "is done in such a matter-of-fact way, which makes absolute sense because Leatherface is doing his job. He's coming in and hanging the meat on the hook, and that's what he does. It's a great decision there because it wrong-foots you; you're not quite sure what you've just seen, who that creature is." Death is matter-of-fact, and the camera moves on.

Teri says the crew were all "dead quiet because everybody was really moved by the scene. I looked for their reaction afterward because I've never done a scene on a meat hook. 'How's it looking so far?' I looked up and they were all just—their mouths were open, they were agape."

"It was horrifying," Bill Vail says. "I couldn't watch it. Pam did such a good job. You were like the lifter in ballet. You're lifting her up, and she's doing all the emoting and all the everything. She was so good, I still get goose bumps. And the room was full of people. There was every crew member there, it was a big frigging deal. And you put her up there, and she was so good about it. I wanted blood coming out of her mouth or something. But it really didn't need it. She just did it. I watched it the first time and went, 'That's disgusting.' And the next time, she started going, and again I had to walk out of the room. It was too much."

The result of all this? "She'll always be known as the meat hook girl. Always," John Dugan says.

Still, for all the horror of this scene, the only blood we see are some old stains splattered across the wall behind Pam.

A story pops up now and then that Tobe wanted more blood in the scene and that he wanted the hook to show through Pam's chest. This story originally came from Bob himself, in a documentary about *Chain Saw*. He objected to Tobe's plan, he said, because this would give the movie an R rating. So Tobe relented. And in an interview Tobe once said, "We wanted PG. We agreed in theory that we might get PG if there was no blood."

But all this is extremely unlikely, for a couple of reasons. I was there, and I don't remember any such argument. Neither do cinematographer Daniel Pearl, sound recordist Ted Nicolaou, nor editor Larry Carroll. Kim Henkel adds, in his way of suggesting that it didn't happen, "If that conversation occurred, I wasn't party to it."

"This is a film about cannibals," Larry says. "It's a film about people who kill people to eat them. That's an automatic R, there's no way around it. I never understood that. I remember talking to Tobe about it, saying, 'Don't they realize?' It was kind of a game with Parsley, because he wanted, somehow, the PG rating. There's just no way, no way this is going to be. I mean you're talking about films like *Mary Poppins*." There was no PG-13 at the time. In any event, the risk seemed more likely that the film would end up with an X. (It was in fact given an R.)

As for blood in general—after all, it is infamous as a splatter movie—*Chain Saw* has surprisingly little. "That's just kind of the way we played it," Kim says. "We were a bit restrained because we were a little bit fearful, but then sort of in the end we decided to throw in a bit. We felt like we had to have an R, that people wouldn't come to see it if we didn't have an R in that genre." Certainly today, anything less than an R is death to a horror movie.

But for all this talk of blood, there is even less gore in the scene as shot than the script calls for: "Kirk hangs nearby nearly stripped of flesh," it reads. "Blood pours from Pams [*sic*] mouth. . . . She coughs and spews a bloody mist clouding the air." But in the movie, Kirk instead lies on a table, his wounds discreetly out of view. And no blood pours or sprays out of Pam's mouth. We do see a bucket under her, suggesting that it is there to catch dripping blood, but it's not something that we see happen.

Even if we had wanted to, we would have had a hard time showing explicit details of the killings such as Kirk's half-flayed body—we could not afford the effects. So our extremely low budget worked to our advantage, making the movie more horrific for what was *not* seen.

Unfortunately for Teri, once she was finished filming, she was still tethered to the production. "They wouldn't release me to go and make some money for a six-week engagement at the Lubbock Dinner Theater," she says. "They needed pickup shots after you guys had finished, and so they said, 'No, I'm sorry, we need you.' They held me over for one day, and that kept me from getting six weeks of work, and I'd already lost my waiting job because of the extension of the filming. I had no money. I was broke, really broke.

I was doing a play with Andy Devine at the Austin Dinner Theater while we were filming, or just after we'd finished filming. I told him about the movie. 'I'm doing this movie about chain saws and meat hooks,' and he's looking at me like I'm insane. I said, 'They want me to do these pickup shots, but I've got an opportunity to go to Lubbock.' And he sat back and he looked at me and he just said, 'Oh, Teri, that thing will never come out of the can.'"

———·———

With Pam taken care of for the moment, writhing in the background, Leatherface moves on to getting Kirk ready for the freezer. As originally conceived, it would have been much more graphic than what we see on-screen, but budget restrictions being what they were, it was toned down even before we started filming it. With its remnant description of Kirk hanging on a hook, the shooting script holds a hint of what Kim and Tobe had first intended. Kim says that as originally written, Leatherface's work on Kirk was much more elaborate. It was "a scene in which somebody was skinned, and their face removed, and Leatherface put it on his face," he says. "So it probably started as a horrific element that simply comes out of the horror of skinning somebody alive and employing parts of that individual. We were making lamps, we're making sculptural pieces, et cetera; why not the face?"

Kim says the change was a practical decision. Maybe there was a bit of concern about an X rating, too.

Even in its stripped-down form, the scene would be a bit tricky to shoot. The camera would be at Bill's feet and would look along his body as I worked on him with the chain saw, though the angle was such that the actual cutting would not be visible. But I would be using a live saw.

During the filming we used the saw in different states. Often Ron Bozman would take the clutch out so the chain was not moving even though the saw itself was roaring and smoking insanely. This was fine for long shots, but when the saw was close to the camera, Ron returned the clutch to let the chain move. In a bit of visual over-caution, most of the time we shot with the clutch in. To reduce the risk, though, we had two chains, a fully sharp one and one with the teeth filed off. We used the sharp one whenever I was cutting something.

This time Tobe wanted to use the sharp chain. I would actually be cutting into the table near Bill's head—the camera could not see the cheat—and Tobe wanted to hear the chain binding as Leatherface cut into Kirk. This was maybe a too close reading of the script, which says, "The chain saw changes pitch as it bites into Kirk's flesh." I thought at the time that this was a bit too realistic—they could just dub in the sound of a binding saw later. But I was too shy to say so to Tobe, so we did it his way.

It was extremely dangerous. The chain saw's bar and chain would be inches from Bill's face. And I was worried that I would hurt him—or worse.

I told Bill that he would be all right, that I would keep him safe. I added, though, that wood chips might hit him in the face, and not to flinch if they did—any shift could move him into the saw and likely kill him. And it would ruin the shot.

He agreed to be still.

In a normal-budget movie none of this would have happened—at least I hope not. First, union and other safety concerns would have dominated the decisions we made about the shot. Second, Bill would have had a stuntman doubling for him on that table. But in our world we did it however we needed to. It seems pretty common in low-budget movies to take chances for the sake of the shot.

All this time, Bill had to look dead. So Tobe gave Dottie a special assignment. "Dottie's job was to make sure I didn't breathe as you were cutting," Bill says. "'You stand right here, and if you see his chest go up and down, you tell me and we'll cut.' So I'm thinking I don't want to do this any longer than necessary, and so I've got to really think about not breathing, really relaxing into the moment as the chain saw's going." I also was hoping for a one-take shot.

I started the saw. It was a great saw—it was the only one we had, and it started every time on the first pull. It was a yellow Poulan 306A, modified with the fuel tank from a Poulan 245 and a muffler from a 245A. Ron says he had initially approached McCulloch about a product placement deal, but he never heard back. We covered the saw's name with a piece of black tape, so as not to raise issues with Poulan. As to its post-filming fate, it had been borrowed for the shoot—from whom unfortunately has been lost to the mists of memory—and afterward was returned to its owner, where it would have lived out its days actually being useful.

But here and now, with the saw roaring, I bent down and started to cut on Bill.

He has a clear memory of that moment, as we all do with near-death experiences. "The sound of it is—it's going into the table, near my head, I don't know, six inches, eight inches," he says. "I could feel splinters hitting me, I could feel the hot oil coming off of the blade, just like little needles sticking me in the side of the face, and I'm trying to relax. It was scary just that it was as close as it was and you had your frigging mask on, so you had no peripheral vision—and it was scary."

This shot was very stupid for us to do. As worried as I was for Bill's safety, I had no idea how dangerous the chain saw really was. As Ron says, "It was a horrendously dangerous piece of gear." And I had never used one before—though I did not let on at the time.

It was not until the following year, when I moved to New England and was heating my house with wood, that I started using a chain saw regularly. Only then did I discover how unpredictable and dangerous it was. Let it bind down too much and it will buck, and no matter how strong you are, it will go where it wants to go. And it will cut anything in its way. If the chain had bound down just right during the filming, the saw probably would have jerked forward and killed Bill. In fact, twenty years later, when I was working on *Mosquito* (a giant bug movie in which my saw and I dispatch some oversized bloodsuckers), I had to cut a door down with a chain saw. That time I asked that the set be cleared of everyone except essential crew. Luckily, nothing went wrong. But as I swung the saw in a subsequent scene, the chain broke, hit the floor, and rebounded up under the safety screen protecting the camera. It hit the first assistant camera operator and wrapped around her leg. It's amazing how tough blue jeans are.

Luckily, nothing went wrong with Bill's scene. I finished the sawing, Tobe yelled "Cut!" and I stepped back. As did Daniel. He looked ashen. Apparently it looked real on camera.

"I remember watching that at the time, just thinking, 'Oh my God, this is some of the most crazy stuff I've ever seen in my life,'" he says. "I do remember, as I was watching the scene, being pulled into it, and just like I was totally inside that camera watching this."

I recall that he muttered some expletive as he stepped away from the camera.

There was a certain stillness on set in those first moments afterward. "The room was just like an operating table," Bill says. "And you're just like—all the nurses, all the assistants, everybody was just here. Then there's the camera, you, me, Pam—that was the world. I thought you had a lot of those reactions in the movie. It always made me laugh because we were almost like The Three Stooges." If so, I was Shemp.

I don't think other people were laughing, though. "It was probably the most horrifying tableau I've seen in movies—ever," Ted says.

There is an interesting sidelight to this story. Just as we were finishing the scene, Sally Nicolaou, the caterer (and Ted's wife), arrived with lunch.

Their three-year-old daughter, Corinna, was with her, as she almost always was. Unfortunately, Corinna spotted Pam on the meat hook. "I was in the living room while we were shooting that scene," Ted says, "and she came running in and skidded to a stop and just went completely white, started screaming and crying, and went running out of the house."

Corinna remembered it in a radio broadcast on Halloween, 2011: "The woman was screaming, then I was screaming, then it was just me screaming," she said.

Ted tried to assure her that no one was being hurt. "We had to bring you out and go 'Oh look, it's just Gunnar. Take off the mask!'" he explains. "She was inconsolable."

Corinna and I were already friends on the set. Because I was isolated from the other actors (at least until the rest of the chain saw family arrived), often the only people I could talk to were assistant cameraman Lou Perryman, when he was not busy, or Corinna, when she was on set with her mother. Corinna would often keep me company sitting on the porch steps. Unlike Frankenstein's monster, however, I did not drop her into a lake to see if she would float.

She had never liked my Leatherface mask. She was sitting with me one day while I waited for a shot setup. When Dottie came to put on my mask, it horrified Corinna. As soon as it covered my face she started screaming. I had Dottie pull it off. "See?" I said, "It's just me." She calmed down. But when I put the mask on again, she started screaming again. I realized she was too young to make the leap, to see my transformation from Gunnar to Leatherface and understand that I was still under the mask. So I made sure she never saw me in the mask after that—at least until the unfortunate meat hook scene.

Still, she continued to come to the set after seeing Teri on the hook, because she also got to know John Dugan and saw him in his Grandpa makeup during the dinner scene. (In her Halloween story she remembered seeing the actors and crew coming out from filming that scene, "gasping for fresh air," which is a pretty accurate description of our condition.)

She did not see *Chain Saw* for many years. But, she says, when she finally did watch it, "Leatherface and Grandpa were like long-lost uncles."

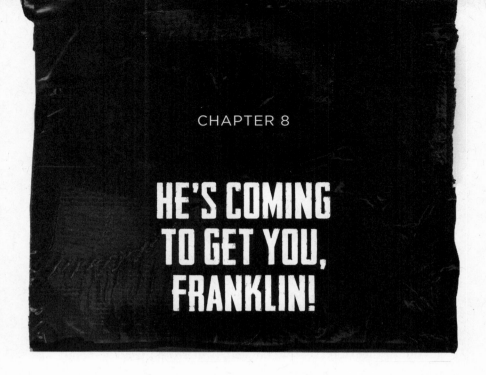

CHAPTER 8

HE'S COMING TO GET YOU, FRANKLIN!

Why do these strangers keep walking into Leatherface's house uninvited? First Kirk goes in and gets punished with a sledgehammer. Then Pam, who gets punished with a meat hook. And now it's Jerry, who's sure to get punished, too. It must be driving poor Leatherface crazy. Or crazier.

Jerry has been wondering where Kirk and Pam are. So he heads out in search of the others, leaving Sally to listen to Franklin's tiresome whining. Jerry finds the house, where he knocks at the door, calling out for his friends. He hears some kind of squawking inside, like an animal. We all know it is Leatherface (the sound was dubbed in later), but Jerry assumes Kirk and Pam are waiting inside, playing some game with him.

And *of course* he walks in. This is a horror movie, after all. This time, though, it's as if Leatherface is baiting Jerry, drawing him in. (Maybe Leatherface is following the old Texas rule for killing intruders—make sure the body is inside the threshold before you call the sheriff.)

Jerry follows the sounds down the hall and into the bloody kitchen, where he sees the meat hook and the butcher-block table, and then hears knocking from inside the chest freezer. He opens it and up pops Pam, now blue from the cold, her body and arms spasming. He jumps back as she flops forward, slumped over the edge of the freezer like a rag doll. Sadly for Jerry, Leatherface charges in, howling, sledge raised, and gives him a double-fisted overhead blow that takes him to the floor. Jerry is about to become sausage.

I was ready for this. After the first two kills it would be a cinch. We set up the first shot, over my shoulder as I swung the sledge down on Allen. To be sure he would fall to the floor violently, as if really hit, a crew member crouched behind him, his hand hooked on Allen's belt. When I swung, he would jerk Allen to the floor.

The camera rolled. I ran in. Jerry turned and screamed. And he ran out of the room, tearing himself loose from the crew member's grasp. He ruined the shot.

"I remember reading about the Stanislavski Method," Allen says. "So I would say my acting came about in my death scene because I remember really getting myself psyched up. I said, 'I don't even want to see what Leatherface looks like until that scene.' So I stayed by myself. I closed my eyes until they said, 'It's showtime.' So I go in, and the scene starts to go, and I give out with one of those shrieks, you know what I mean. And then I guess I start running. Tobe called me and said, 'Great, great scream, but you got to wait until he's in the shot with you, Allen. You know, with the sledgehammer.'"

So much for wanting to keep the acting real. We reshot Jerry's death, this time without Allen's real shock. But the look on his face and his horrified scream are convincing. It's as if he's not even acting, though he is.

I do not want to make too much fuss about the acting in horror movies, since it is not really what they are about. There was a time when about the only people making horror were those with little money and a determination to make a name for themselves. So actors were either beginners looking for a start, or old-timers looking for a modest payday. There are, of course, plenty of mainstream actors who got their start in horror—consider Renée Zellweger and Matthew McConaughey, who both appeared in *Texas Chainsaw Massacre: The Next Generation* near the beginning of their careers. Nowadays horror is popular with mainstream producers, so we do at times hope for some "real" actors. But, historically, acting isn't the strength of low-budget film. Directors are looking for someone who will show up on time and put up with the misery. We were lucky with *Chain Saw*—we had some fine acting in it, particularly from Jim Siedow and Paul Partain. And the rest of us certainly carried our share.

———•———

Having killed Jerry, Leatherface tosses Pam back into the freezer, leaves Jerry's body on the kitchen floor, and runs to the living room window. He hits the hanging chicken cage with his hand as he passes. The chicken squawks and clucks. Leatherface pulls the curtains back and peers out into the setting sun as he checks to the right and then to the left several times. No one is there. He seems safe for the moment.

But he is upset. He paces back and forth, sits down, and begins to fuss and worry. He puts his head in his hands, then pats his little leather face. He runs his tongue over his serrated teeth. He stares off into the distance with his blank eyes, as if he is almost thinking. This was my—well, Leatherface's—first real close-up. Then Leatherface looks away, as if he has decided something.

Tobe did give me some instructions for this scene, beyond just blocking out my movements: You're worried. Where are these people coming from? You're being invaded. What are you going to do? And slap the chicken cage when you go by—let's get some more movement in the shot.

I knew that this would be my best chance to show Leatherface's state of mind—my one chance to "act," in the conventional sense. I do not know how many takes we shot—not many, probably— but I do remember the intense concentration. This time I was not charged up on adrenaline. I was calm. I wanted to get it right. Once I sat down for the close-up, I focused on running my tongue over my teeth and on my blank stare. I was so focused that I had no sense of where the camera was.

The scene is powerful, a still moment in all the craziness. And it makes its point. The audience does get a sense of Leatherface's inner workings, limited as they might be.

"This is one of my most favorite scenes in the whole thing," art director Bob Burns once said, "when he gets all perturbed because things aren't going the way they're supposed to. He's just this lost soul, because things just aren't going right. Things are not going right at all. It's just wonderful."

"Leatherface is so pathetic," says John Landis, director of *An American Werewolf in London* (1981). "Even though you see someone like Leatherface, who clearly is a maniacal, homicidal psychopath, you do have empathy for him. He's a tragic figure."

It is a curious thing about *Chain Saw* fans. Many of them have a sympathetic view of Leatherface. It is as if they appreciate that he has elements of both the human and the inhuman. To some he is even loveable, though I do not see that part myself.

"There's a childlike quality to Leatherface," Doug Bradley says. "I don't know whether this is where people's identification comes in. There's an innocence to him. It's not that he's just the crazed killer, there's almost a feeling that he's not quite sure why he's doing what he's doing, maybe isn't even comfortable with what he's doing. Also in the context of family, he's the obedient child."

I think the key to that perception lies in this scene. This is the only time we see him really worried, even a little frightened. Later scenes with the family will fill in our sense of him a bit, especially his fear, though not so obviously.

"It's funny," Stuart Gordon director of *Re-Animator* says. "I teach some at film schools, and the kids will say things like 'Well, this guy doesn't have any lines, so you can get anybody to do it.' No. If he doesn't have any lines you're going to need somebody who's really fantastic to play that part because acting isn't about speaking. Acting is about doing and conveying emotions and things physically. It's a visual medium." Thank you, Stuart.

——·——

What Leatherface has decided, of course, is that he will not wait till the next intruder invades the house, but rather he will go after them.

Before Franklin and Sally meet Leatherface, they have an extended squabble at the van. Sally wants to search for the others—without Franklin. But Franklin insists they go back to the gas station for help. He rolls over to the van and panics when he sees the keys are gone. He starts blasting its horn, and the two scream at each other as they tussle over the flashlight. Franklin is extremely irritating throughout this scene, just like Paul was off camera.

And Tobe, meanwhile, was making their conflict worse, in the hope of getting it on-screen. "Tobe would come up and tell me that Paul said something about me," Marilyn once said of filming this scene. "And then Tobe was going to Paul, saying, 'Marilyn said something about you,' getting us really upset with each other, so we're doing this scene that didn't require any acting at all. I was ready to kill him." Reportedly, by this point the two of them were not otherwise speaking to each other.

In an interview with John Bloom for a *Texas Monthly* article, Paul explained some of the tension. Bloom writes, quoting Paul, "'Yeah, she was pissed,' he says. 'She thought I was screwing up the scene. But they were writing me new dialogue on the spot—I think on purpose. . . . We kept doing it over and over. And I was a young, inexperienced actor who didn't realize that it wasn't like theater—you didn't have to stay in character all the time.'"

The audience sees that anger on the screen. Sally pushes Franklin in his wheelchair through the mesquite brake, made more difficult by the lack of a path. They bicker. But most of this dialogue was unscripted. When Franklin whines, "Push down! Get back and push down!" that really was just Paul nagging Marilyn.

And all the takes did not help matters at all. As Paul once joked, "Take four hundred twelve. Just push it, Marilyn."

I waited quietly as they approached. For days I had wanted Paul dead. I despised this whining loser. I fired up my chain saw, stepped in front of him, and brought it down across his body, then finished him off with a deep, satisfying thrust into his chest. He screamed and shuddered, and his blood spattered up on me. He dropped his flashlight, and it hit the ground like some severed body part.

I felt good.

The kill was fake. But my feelings were real. Like Marilyn, I wanted to kill Paul. So I got plenty of satisfaction. Aside from acting out my hate, I knew that once he was dead he was off the set. Forever. I liked that thought.

Looking back these years later, I realize that I, too, had been caught up in the trap Tobe had set for us, even though I knew at the time what he was doing. The emotion bound up in this kill was part of my failing to distinguish reality from acting.

Both Paul and Marilyn were terrified when we shot the scene. Paul said later that neither of them had ever seen me in my "stuff," as he called it. "And," he added, "that guy is pretty scary when you see him in the middle of the night coming out at you with a chain saw going."

"I was very scared, very terrified," Marilyn says. "You were so big and the face was so awful—and also the noise of the chain saw. So yeah, it was very, very scary. I didn't even know you could be that tall. You just looked like you never ended. I think where I jump every time is when I'm pushing Franklin down that hill and Leatherface bursts through the bushes, because it scares me. It really scares me; I'm still jumping."

"The one place where there's real splatter in *Chain Saw* is this moment," boom operator Wayne Bell says. "So we wanted blood to gush, to splatter on Leatherface."

To get that blood splatter, Tobe crouched on Paul's right with a cup of Bob's stage blood—Karo syrup and food coloring—in his hand. Dottie Pearl did the same on the left. The camera was behind Paul, looking up at me. Then, as I slashed, they took mouthfuls of the blood and spit it at me. Even Wayne got into the act, spraying blood on me as if he were making a raspberry. "For me this is just a delight," he says. "I care nothing about horror movies, but this was pretty playful." Toward the end of the splattering, I saw Tobe toss the last bit of blood in his cup on me. It is visible on-screen as a red splotch on the left side of Leatherface's apron.

"Tobe and Dotty Pearl spitting blood," Marilyn says. "Talk about million-dollar special effects! But it looked damn good and damn real. I was laughing, that was the funniest part in the movie."

The funniest part, maybe, was that this was the bloodiest scene in the movie. Otherwise, as editor Larry Carroll says, "It turned out to be a gore-less splatter film."

It is interesting how people see this scene—and much of the rest of the movie. When it came out on video in the 1980s, people complained to me that all the good stuff—the gore—had been edited out. So I watched it. Nope, it was all there. These people just remembered its being much more explicit than it was.

One time a fan came up to me at a horror convention and said, "*Chain Saw* had the best special effects I've ever seen in a horror movie. Why can't they do it as well anymore?"

That was because there were no special effects in the movie, I said.

"No, no!" he said. "I *saw* you cut that guy in the wheelchair in half."

Nope. What he did see, though, was Leatherface in close-up, raising the roaring chain saw and thrusting it forward while Franklin screams. The rest of the kill is a series of shots from behind Franklin of Leatherface slowly slashing and stabbing with the chain saw, as if cutting through something. Blood splatters up on him the whole time. But the camera never shows the saw cut anything.

No matter how much I argued the point, he would not believe me. I finally suggested he watch the movie again to see how much gore was really in it. I think all of us from *Chain Saw* have run into this over the years, including Ron Bozman. "That's a testament to the power of it all," he says.

"It's great," Stuart Gordon says. "It leaves the worst of the carnage to the audience's imagination. And what you imagine is far worse than anything that could be put on-screen. It's very participatory, and I think that's the thing about *Texas Chain Saw* that's really great: it lets the audience be part of the process."

That participation was so total that at the time of *Chain Saw*'s release, the *Philadelphia Inquirer* ran stories reporting that audience members were so disgusted by what they saw that they were throwing up in the theater and demanding their money back; their imaginations were too much for them.

Chain Saw exemplifies—with a twist—the concept of hot and cool media, a reference to the degree of participation of the audience. Radio is a hot medium because the listeners must use their imagination to fill the visual gaps. Movies, on the other hand, are cool, because everything is on the screen and the viewers just sit back and let it wash over them. Except for movies like *Chain Saw*. Within this otherwise cool medium, it is pretty warm.

And that may be one key to the power of the movie—the unseen is much greater, and gorier, than the seen. If the movie had been more explicit, likely it would not been as involving, or as enduring.

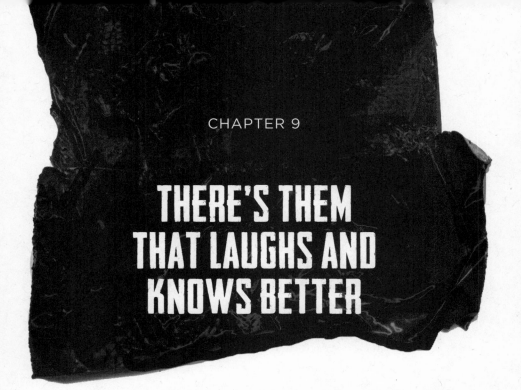

CHAPTER 9

THERE'S THEM THAT LAUGHS AND KNOWS BETTER

By this point I was losing all sense of time. The days were so long and unrelenting that, looking back, I do not know when one day of filming ended and the next began. I remember that we were now on set twelve to sixteen hours a day, seven days a week. And I remember the temperature to be at a hundred or worse every day, with that infamous Central Texas humidity (weather records suggest it wasn't quite that bad, but that's how it felt). Others recall that we, or at least they, had Sundays off, or that the days were shorter.

Some also seemed to have enough free time to party after the day's shooting—Kim Henkel remembers at times camping out all night at an actor's house to "catch them when they came in so we could drag them on set." Myself, I had only enough time to go home, clean up, and get some sleep so I could get back on set on time the next day. In fact, I had no social life during the filming. My housemate had worked on *Lovin' Molly* himself, and had been pleased that I got a part in *Chain Saw*, but I never even had time to talk to him about it till almost the end of filming. I was so caught up in work that though his girlfriend moved in with us right after I started working on the movie, she had been living with us for a month before I realized it.

Anyway, I can safely say that the days were long, hot, and tiring, and they ran into each other. Allen Danziger remembers that we had an air-conditioned RV on set for a while, a place to rest and prepare for the next scene, which must have been nice. But by the time we moved to the chain saw family house—that is, by the time I was filming—this perhaps mythical RV had been returned to wherever it may have come from, and we were now reduced to a beat-up, barely running thing with no air-conditioning, which was a real chore for Ron to move when we needed to clear it for a shot. Kim Henkel doesn't even remember the nice RV. "I only remember this old wreck of a thing that we had, or we kept trying to keep going," he says. It belonged to investor Bob Kuhn, who would have to come out and fix it whenever it broke down.

Because it had no air-conditioning, and because the sun beat down on it, the heat inside was brutal. We stayed in it long enough to dress and do our makeup. And then we got the hell out. Usually an RV or trailer is essential to surviving on location, and a low-budget movie is lucky to have one. It needs to be a place where actors can concentrate and recharge. To maintain quiet, nonessential crew access is often restricted. Still, the RV is not always so peaceful. On one movie I did later a "producer" arrived with an attractive woman in tow. He told us to leave because they needed the bedroom to record a song. We refused. On another shoot, our still photographer was constantly taking pictures in the RV, telling us to move here or there and pose with someone who was not supposed to be there. Unfortunately, I had a lot of dialogue in that movie and needed a quiet place to concentrate. I finally told her that there would be no photography and no conversation in the RV. Life after that was blissfully relaxed. At least in our *Chain Saw* trailer we had no problem inside with unnecessary noise or distractions: it was uninhabitable.

But there was one great thing about our RV: It was here that I learned about how Tobe and Kim came up with *The Texas Chain Saw Massacre*. It was late at night—with the Franklin kill we would be shooting at night till the last scene. The three of us sat inside while we waited for a scene setup. This time of night, the RV could be quite pleasant. With no sun, the box would lose its heat, and after a few hours of darkness, the open windows and door might even let a bit of a breeze through to cool it down. Compared to my usual perch, the porch steps, the seats were oh-so-soft. I remember staring out the windshield at the chain saw family house as we talked.

I asked Tobe and Kim where they had come up with the ideas for *Leatherface*, as we called it then. Tobe said that the bone-and-skin furniture and Leatherface's mask had been inspired by Ed Gein, a farmer in Wisconsin who had been caught in the late 1950s after he had killed and gutted the owner of the local hardware store. Gein had been a quiet man whose neighbors thought they knew him well. He also had the habit of digging people up from their graves, including his own mother, whose remains he put back in her bed. More to the point, he had made masks and lots of skin-and-bone artifacts, including bowls and furniture coverings, from these dug-up bodies.

There was another Gein element in the early conception of the script. "One thing about Ed Gein that was interesting," Kim says, "was the at least apparent normalcy of his life to those who are looking in from the outside, unless of course you got too terribly close." The Cook in *Chain Saw* has a kind of Ed Gein normalcy when seen from a distance.

This seems to be all that Tobe knew about Gein when he and Kim were writing the script. In an interview some years later, Tobe said that his Wisconsin relatives, who had lived near Gein's farm, had told him these stories, but neither he nor they knew Gein's name. He joked that he didn't even know that *Chain Saw* was based on "Ed Gein" till years after he had made the movie.

(Gein was the inspiration for Robert Bloch's 1958 novel *Psycho*, which Hitchcock adapted for his 1960 movie, and for the Jame Gumb [Buffalo Bill] character who skins women in *The Silence of the Lambs*, though the Hannibal Lecter character himself is not based on Gein.)

Beyond using Gein as the inspiration for Leatherface's mask and his family's home decor, Tobe said, he and Kim had decided to just fill the movie with everything that had ever scared them in horror movies.

One of those elements was the urban fear of country folk, who, to the city dweller, stood outside of civilization and its strictures. "I'm pretty sure we were convinced that if our cars ever broke down between cities, the rednecks would just have their way with us," Daniel Pearl says. "I always thought this film was sort of an extension, this was sort of taking that paranoia even just one step further, where they would wind up eating us." Sort of *Deliverance* on steroids.

"Now we escape to get out into the country, where we feel safe from civilization," Tobe said recently in an unpublished interview with Italian writer Paolo Zelati. "But there used to be a real threat. Back in the early part of the twentieth century you would go out and get killed out in the country. And EC Comics depicted a lot of that too. I remember a lot of night scenes out in the woods and out in the countryside. They used to be scary. They used to just be the icon of scary. Being out there, being isolated, before cell phones existed, even before telephones existed, but to be out there and there's no one out there to help you. So Leatherface—the isolation of that house, even to the point they were off the mainstream completely, what we now call 'off the grid.' They had their own little generator. They didn't want someone coming around and checking the electric meter."

Tobe has also said that the idea for using a chain saw came when he was Christmas shopping at Montgomery Ward (at the time a kind of poor-man's Sears). The store was so jammed with shoppers, he said, that he panicked. He tried to get out, but could not move against the crowd. He realized that he was in the hardware department and saw a display of chain saws nearby. And he had that unholy inspiration, the seed that grew into *The Texas Chain Saw Massacre*: if he had a chain saw he could cut his way out. The story is too good not to be true.

Beyond the mask and the skin-and-bone stuff, *Chain Saw* is not about Gein. It is also not based on a series of killings in Texas just before we made the movie, although one can see how this misunderstanding developed, since it comes from Kim Henkel himself. In a curious example of memory gone awry, Kim says that part of the inspiration for the chain saw family came from the Candy Man Murders, particularly serial killer Elmer Wayne Henley, Jr., who, with Dean Arnold Corll and David Owen Brooks, helped capture, torture, rape, and kill twenty-eight teenage boys in Houston in the early 1970s. After his arrest, he reportedly said he was going to "face it like a man," a curiously deluded and conventional bit of moral high ground for a killer of boys. It was a stance that Kim says was "very much a part of the whole *Chain Saw* thing, with the characters behaving this way." Indeed it is just the sort of line that we might hear from the Cook, who says, "I just can't take no pleasure in killing. There's just some things you gotta do. Don't mean you have to like it."

But, in spite of Kim's recollection, Elmer Wayne Henley could not have been an inspiration for *Chain Saw*. Henley confessed to his crimes on August 8, 1973. By then we were already filming, the script long since written and the Cook's character well established. According to the shooting schedule, I was hanging Pam on the meat hook that day.

Whatever their inspiration, when it came time for Kim and Tobe to write their script—based minimally on a real person and not at all on real events—they withdrew to Tobe's house in Austin to work.

Kim says that they decided to write a horror movie because of budget. "If you have relatively little money, what are your possibilities?" he says. "The clear answer was some sort of genre piece. Horror was the easiest because we felt that we didn't have to have any names in the cast, production values weren't nearly so important as in some other realms, so it became the natural choice."

In developing the story, they tossed around a lot of ideas. But one constant kept coming up. "I think we were kind of rooted in *Grimm's Fairy Tales* in some ways," Kim says, "trying to go back to look at what those stories were about, in that they tend to deal with fundamental issues that human beings struggle with over the course of millenniums. If you can get to the core of what those tales are trying to do, then you try to address those issues."

And the tale that kept popping up? "Hansel and Gretel," a story of trespass, of a brother and sister lost in the deep woods coming to the house of a cannibalistic witch. The house is made of gingerbread, and the two help themselves to a meal before the witch lures them inside. "It was one of the key things," Kim says. "You lure the potential victims to the ghoul's lair with gingerbread cookies and the like. There was a whole process of luring the people to the home. So it was very much rooted in 'Hansel and Gretel.'" Except maybe for the chain saw.

Kim also saw the story as a kind of urban-mythology tale. "People set out," he says. "They violate a code, in this case they trespass on private property, so they violate some fundamental underlying . . . they unleash the forces of opposition against themselves, and it goes from there."

"I wasn't schooled in horror, didn't have a background in horror, was not a fan of horror, particularly," Kim says. "So my approach to it wasn't so much 'It's horror.' It was more for the social side of it. The horror to me, taken seriously, was just something I couldn't quite deal with, so I guess I approached it in a way that was maybe a little different."

There is another element related to this trespassing theme, Kim says. "The family can also be seen as victims. They were being trespassed on, another insult after having their livelihoods taken."

This creates ambivalence for the *Chain Saw* audience. We naturally empathize with and fear for the travelers. From that point of view, the family is the antagonist, the monster terrorizing these five. But we can look at it from the other side, from that of the family—and the movie certainly invites us to. Now we see that it is the family who are put upon. They are the ones who are just trying to survive when the young travelers—the antagonists in this framing—violate their home. The travelers trespass. They enter the house uninvited—even after being warned off at the gas station by the Cook: "You boys don't want to go messin' around in some old house. Those things is dangerous. You're liable to get hurt." This explains why Leatherface runs to the window after killing Jerry. He's not wondering whether there is any more meat out there. He's worried about why these people are invading his house. This also helps one understand why some view him as sympathetic.

Some early script elements did not make it into the final draft. "When we sat down and we talked about the story ideas, the basic structure of *Chain Saw* we sort of laid out," Kim says. "But we came to a bit of an impasse, and the impasse was that Tobe had an idea about whoever occupied this house as being some sort of electronic being, for want of a better expression, not of this earth, almost insubstantial, almost a whirling orbit of protons and neutrons flying around or something." This echoes an element from Tobe's earlier *Eggshells*. According to Wayne Bell, that movie—which has been publicly screened in America only once since its original release, so we'll have to take his word for it—includes at its center "something supernatural, otherworldly, a presence that lives in this house."

"I took the position, basically," Kim continues, "that what really is scary is us. *We're* what is frightening—human beings.

So then [Tobe] came back at me with the chain saw guy, and I thought that was terrific. Then we added the whole thing with the mask. The changing of characters is not that he'd been tortured as a child and turned out badly, but that basically he is who he wears. He becomes the persona of that mask, so the monster is us. There's of course the whole Jekyll and Hyde aspect of that process. Also there's a great short story by Vonnegut ["Who Am I This Time?"]. It was about sort of a milquetoast character who was a nobody and nothing until he stepped on the stage and was given a role, and then he could be anything." In the story, the character of Harry Nash is powerful and somehow more real only on stage, interestingly, raising questions as to whether a role—and thus, theatrically, a mask—reveals the true self, something that I think applies to Leatherface.

Early in the story development, Leatherface had the mask, which would make sense if he were, as Tobe said, inspired by Ed Gein's masks. "It was probably a very practical kind of thing," Kim says, the result of deciding to have Leatherface carve off someone's face and put it on like a mask. The skinning scene did not make it into the movie, though the mask did.

"We talked through the whole thing several times," Kim says. "And we'd go back and refine and whittle it down, but as a conversation. Then once we felt we were fairly solid, I'd just go out to the kitchen table, and I had a little typewriter there, and I'd start typing, writing scenes. I'd write a scene and then bring it in to Tobe and we'd review it.

"Our criterion for whether it was working is whether I could keep him chuckling. I mean it's a peculiar sort of humor, of course. Many, many years ago I was living in L.A. and I used to hang out at the old Improv that was on Melrose. I ran into Andy Kaufman there, and it turned out he was a big *Chain Saw* fan. The one thing he wanted to know was if, when we wrote it and when we made it, did we think it was funny, were our intentions to make it funny. So I told him that we thought it was funny as hell, but at the same time, we wanted to make it very scary."

"You can't laugh," Tobe said in his Zelati interview. "At the time, that kind of ironic, dark humor was not humorous. In fact, mixing those elements inside that horror, for some reason it really made it; I think it simulated insanity in a way that portraying insanity had not been successful in films before. In most films the portrayal of insanity, at least then, was an actor acting insane."

The black, bitter humor in *Chain Saw* lies deeply enough under the surface that many have had to watch the movie several times before it becomes apparent.

And then came the rewrites, the part that makes the script actually work. In this case, as one can see from the shooting script, the polishing and refining continued right into the production.

"We cleaned it up and filled in holes that would make it work more effectively," Kim says. "I think maybe in the original draft we didn't make a direct connection between, let's say, the closing of the slaughterhouse—it's sort of implied—that set these things in motion, certain things that I think maybe were not clearly drawn in those first drafts. Story-wise we felt like we needed to provide some kind of solid linchpins there. It provides the kind of details that make the experience particularly riveting. Just exploring the kinds of things that make audiences very, very uncomfortable were very effective there. For instance, at the end of that final dinner table sequence when they've got her down over that pail and they are going to crack her head, they don't just get a big hammer and whack at her. The whole family joins in, and it becomes this mad, chaotic, bungled attempt, but one that's excruciating and painful, that's played out in a kind of detail and with a level of craziness that I just don't think you ordinarily see."

Kim and Tobe wrote the script in January and February of 1973. Once it was complete, the movie moved along fairly quickly. They were in production that summer.

Daniel Pearl's reaction when he read the screenplay: "I had chills up my spine," he says. "I locked the door when I was reading it."

If only other screenplays were like that. There is a real lesson here for the rest of us who are making low-budget horror movies. When you are starting out, the script is the least expensive part of your movie. A good one will cost you the same as a lousy one—nothing. It can be different on a bigger-budget shoot, where the producers pay for the script and its rewrites. But on a low-budget horror movie, likely the writer is also making the movie. So why not write a good script and give your movie a chance to overcome its other limitations? I once worked on a very low-budget horror movie, *Gimme Skelter* (2007). I would guess that the entire budget was not more than $10,000. But it was a very good movie, partly because it had a great script. The characters were real, the audience cared for them, the story was engaging, and the movie was scary.

Sometimes it seems that low-budget moviemakers are in such a hurry that they undermine their chance to make something that people will want to watch. They rush into production before their scripts are ready—sometimes even before they really have a script. But if they would calm down and reread the script with some distance and then rewrite it, and maybe a third and fourth time, they will make a more engaging, more believable, and more frightening movie. They will also have a more shoot-able movie, since every time they rework the script they are rethinking and working out production kinks. Otherwise they are just wasting their money—and the audience's time.

I once received a script that drove me away within a page. The playlist at the beginning described the primary characters:

JACOB: high school quarterback, handsome
BRITNEY: his girlfriend, big-breasted blonde
RYAN: high school running back, Jacob's best friend
MADISON: his girlfriend, big-breasted brunette
DOOLEY: high school lineman, comic sidekick
ASHLEY: his girlfriend, big-breasted redhead

These are not characters. They barely rise to being clichés. For all the talk that the chain saw family's victims were merely "fodder characters," they were much more realistic and believable than this bunch. All the characters in *Chain Saw* had substance to them, and the audience cared about them. Even Franklin. Especially Franklin. And its story is compelling because Tobe and Kim took the time to hammer it out, to think about it and make it mean something—to give it such resonance that nearly forty years later we are still talking about it and still laughing under our breath at its insanity.

CHAPTER 10

I THOUGHT *YOU* WAS IN A HURRY!

I am glad I spent so much time running in the back field. I did it almost every day, whenever my mask was off and I knew I had twenty or thirty minutes free. It improved my wind, of course, but more important, it helped me with my balance in those high-heeled boots. Or so I thought.

The hardest part for me in making this movie was the chase. It was actually two chases: Sally's initial run after Leatherface kills Franklin, ending when she arrives at the chain saw family house; and then moments later when she dives out the second-floor window and runs to the gas station. Certainly it was no walk in the woods for Marilyn, either. But it was also hard for the crew, at least technically. A lot of their challenges came directly from the tight budget, starting with the film and the lighting.

Because we could not afford to shoot using the standard 35mm film, we used 16mm, which was cheaper at every stage—camera rental, film, processing, editing, and lab. Because of the grain problems with blowing up the final print to 35mm, Daniel Pearl had chosen the least grainy film available. It was also the slowest, ASA-25 color positive. It needed a lot of light—four times as much as the normal, and too grainy, color negative film of the time, according to Daniel. (Today's ASA-800 cameras require only one-sixteenth of the light our old film did.)

This slow film generally was not too much of a hindrance in daylight—though there were a few daytime challenges—but at night it could be a big problem, especially for us, because we did not have many lights. The budget limited us to two 5-kilowatt and one 10-kilowatt lights. For the night shooting, Daniel's crew set up two towers, one with the two 5-Ks, the other with the 10-K. By comparison, when I was shooting a day scene on *Texas Chainsaw 3D* (2013), the cinematographer used a 10-K just as a fill light on me. Dealing with the lighting and the exposure was the hardest part of the whole shoot for Daniel. We really did not have enough light to shoot the night sequences.

"We were shooting at night, one, two, three stops underexposed," Ron Bozman says, "And yet it's all there. It's all there."

"The thing is that we didn't actually know too much at that time, so I didn't know what I was missing," Daniel says. "I'd never lit anything that big at night. I'd never seen lights that big before. I thought I could burn a city down. They looked like they'd unleash nuclear power in my hands."

The lighting, inadequate as it was for our purposes, did cause another problem. We blew a transformer on a nearby power pole. Luckily for us, the power company quickly sent a lineman out to repair it, even though it was the middle of the night, so we were not delayed too long. We invited the lineman to stay and watch the filming. Having him there made me nervous, because I thought I must have looked pretty stupid, running through the woods with my mask and chain saw. Still, he stuck with us till we broke up at first light, so likely he enjoyed the show.

Our budget limited us to forty feet of dolly track, which meant that the patch of woods we were filming in—and lighting—was tiny. We shot most of the chase in that small area.

"We used that same stretch of track, and we shot facing off of one side of the track going left to right, and then we shot going right to left," Daniel says. "Then we turned the camera around and shot off the opposite side of the track, and went right to left and left to right. Obviously there are other parts of that chase, but a lot of the detail work in that chase, the running with the limbs passing in the foreground, a lot of the actual stuff where the camera is moving in the chase, was shot off that one section of dolly track, which is quite a creative, good low-budget technique. You can't tell one tree from another anyhow, so just get that one section of the forest that's ideal for you and just milk it, which is what we did."

Add different focal-length lenses to the shooting mix, and Daniel could pull a large number of very different looking shots in that forty feet.

And it worked. "I have to say that when I watch it, it's quite phenomenal what we accomplished," Daniel says.

Daniel did have one mishap while filming the chase. His dolly grip had only about two steps at the start of a take to get the dolly moving to match my running speed. One time, apparently, he was not fast enough. "I got behind on the dolly," Daniel says, "which forced me to pan more to the right, which brought my elbow back off the dolly and hit a tree, racing through there, which then put the shock in the elbow back through the camera, which smacked me in the eye. I believe I got a black eye from that."

It is nice to know that we actors were not the only ones getting banged up.

A decision that may have made shooting the chase a bit easier for the crew was that Marilyn and I were almost never in the same shot together. I think that we had shared the frame when we started shooting the chase. But Marilyn was a slow runner, and that ended quickly. Not that I've ever been fast, myself—this was the first time in my life that I had outrun someone. But that difference in speed was causing problems, and it was dangerous for Marilyn. I was almost blind in the mask, was wearing slick-soled, high-heeled boots, and was carrying a chain saw—all the while running in the woods at night. So I was afraid of overrunning her and felt relieved when they split us up for the shooting.

One moment in the chase in which we are in the same frame is when Sally's hair catches in the brush and she stops to pull herself free. Leatherface is supposed to come into the shot just as Sally breaks free and runs off. But Marilyn did not run off—she kept pulling on her hair. I assumed it was because she wanted to linger in front of the camera a bit for her close-up. So, trying not to ruin the shot by killing her, I began trimming the brush with my saw—it seemed consistent with Leatherface's mentality—to give her time to get moving. It worked. She broke free, and I was able to resume the chase.

Of course, I was wrong about why Marilyn had hesitated. Her hair was actually caught in the brush, and she could not get free. This only made her fear worse. "Oh, God, I thought you were going to really hurt me," she says. "When we were in the mesquite bushes and my hair was getting caught, well, you couldn't see through your stupid mask and—I don't know if that was a trick or not, but I was told you couldn't see, and you couldn't see where you were going. So I had to hurry and get out of there fast. I'm thinking, 'He's really going to get me.' Plus you were damn scary! First of all, the chain saw, the noise, the harshness of just 'Action! Cut!' is all you heard all night." This time they were not lying when they told her that I could barely see.

There was a frightening instant when my blindness, the slick boots, the chain saw, the woods, and the darkness all converged, and I fell with the saw. I had decided to make a sharp left turn at the end of the trail to add a new bit of movement to the chase. Maybe I was thinking I was wearing football cleats, because when I shifted my weight and set my feet they went out from under me. As I went down, I pitched the chain saw up. I landed on my back, and the saw went up somewhere past the lights. I looked around frantically for it, but could see nothing. Even if the saw had not gone up into the darkness, I think that my mask would have kept me from spotting it. I rolled onto my side and curled up, my arms over my head. The chain saw landed beside me, still running.

Luckily, Marilyn was not in the shot with me, or I could have injured her. But she was close by, standing in the dark waiting for her turn on camera. She could not see where the saw went, either. "We were all kids, it was dark at night, we didn't know what we were doing, we were using a real chain saw," she says, recalling how stupid we were. "It's just us waiting for the saw to come down on our heads. For heaven's sake, you could have lost a limb. And we were at that age where nothing's going to get us, and the director and writer were thinking, *If it does, it will look good in our movie.*"

This was, I think, the only time in the filming when I was genuinely frightened.

My fall had consequences moments later on-screen. With Leatherface close behind, Sally spots the chain saw family house and heads for the back door. Then she turns and runs around the corner, toward the front. Right behind her comes Leatherface, roaring along with his saw. I was supposed to make a sharp turn at the back door and follow Marilyn. But I was not about to let myself fall a second time. So I decided to cheat the turn, to somehow do it in a way that would keep me safe. I also knew that there was no way for me to hide the cheat—no matter what, it would be obvious to the audience.

I decided to point to it, to make the cheat so obvious that the audience would see it as just part of Leatherface's way of running. So, as I came into the frame, I did an exaggerated skid on one foot, revved the saw overhead, and continued on my way. It was, I thought at the time, my Keystone Kops moment.

This is one of Ed Neal's favorite scenes, though to him it is more of a Three Stooges moment. "I always point it out to people," he says. "'Watch this! You've got to see this. Pay attention! Pay attention!' She's such an athlete and, like a wounded antelope, sprints perfectly around the edge. Here you come, and you're charging, and you're so large that you can't possibly *be* the antelope. It's almost like a cartoon *wup-wup-wup-wup!* It's just a magic little moment where the character is so pure that, yes, he's this psychotic person that kills people, but he's still a large man who's not athletic. To me it's this little light moment that gives the audience just a second to catch their breath."

And it gave me a chance to not fall.

Then, once I chased Marilyn around to the front of the house, things got really complicated and slow.

I think it was the drugs.

Caterer Sally Nicolaou arrived with our lunch before we filmed my chasing Marilyn into the house. And Sally had a special treat, a couple of large flats of brownies. I assume she told us that this was her special marijuana recipe. (Maybe she was inspired by the ready availability of the crop growing in the back field.)

I know I ate a couple—or more. They were really good. Smoothed me right out. And then, when I got the munchies, I ate a few more. Whatever food was left over from lunch on any given day became craft services—the snacks on set to keep our energy up. And in this case, the leftover brownies were our craft services. So for the rest of the night every time we wanted a snack, we went back to the brownies.

I don't really know who was stoned. I know I was, and I'm sure a lot of people were, but few have admitted it to me. As Wayne Bell says, "I don't remember the marijuana brownies, but that could be testament to their effectiveness."

I know that Ron was not happy. "I didn't have any, thank God," he says. "After dinner I was looking around, and people were getting more and more bizarre, and somebody said Sally put some weed in the brownies. God, that was the night you were cutting in the door. I was so mad."

"I got out there and everyone except Ron Bozman is completely zonked," editor Larry Carroll says. "Just almost staggering around, bumping into trees, stoned, and we still had a ton of stuff to shoot. So I became the first AD because Ron and I were the only two that were still straight. We just worked getting shots together, and getting people in the right place, and sort of moving Tobe from here to there. That was a long night, too."

Everything slowed down after that. Setting up the next shot, Leatherface's run up to the door and his cutting it down, was interminable. A friend who was visiting the set that night says that while I waited, I was sitting in a chair on the porch, my mask on, my feet up on the railing. He swears I was chanting, "Time has no meaning, time has no meaning, time has no meaning." I sort of remember that.

Though, of course, setups were always slow. "We would spend hours each day waiting for Tobe and Kim to make up their minds on what they were going to shoot," sound recordist Ted Nicolaou says. "It was unusual for a low-budget film."

"They would block these things out and then they'd get into the reality of the situation and they'd go, 'Uhhh, how we gonna do that?'" Ed Neal says. "Then, of course, the cameraman would have some input, and the sound guy would go, 'Well, what if you do this?' Then even the clapper loader would go, 'Well, I think you ought to do that.' Because they were always trying to figure out how the heck they were going to get the shot."

I do sometimes wonder if this chronic slowness was related to our landlord's extracurricular gardening. Supposedly everyone stayed away from it during work hours, but I am not sure. And I am not the only one who has entertained this notion. "I thought that was part of the reason for the confused discussions every day of what we were about to shoot," Ted says.

Some hours into our brownie-fueled shooting, several of us waited in the dining room of the house while Tobe and Daniel were at the head of the stairs, thrashing out how to light the landing. It would not be visible for long—Sally and Leatherface would run through it a couple of times, and I think it is on-screen a total of twelve seconds. But Tobe and Daniel, as I recall, spent more than an hour arguing over the lighting. Finally, as we sat there sweating, Dottie Pearl spoke up. "I think we are all dead," she said, "and sitting in hell." When you're stoned, that sounds totally profound.

We were finally ready. In the shot, I was to cut through the door, kick it in, and then, after stepping inside and glancing around for Sally, pursue her up the stairs. Because we had only one sacrificial door, we had two cameras running—one to catch the action from outside, and the other, run by Daniel, inside on the floor looking up at the door.

I was nervous, though not so much about the live saw—I had already seen it at its worst. Rather, I worried that I was too stoned to remember what to do. I knew I could get through the door all right, but after that could I hold myself together long enough to chase her up the stairs?

Marilyn was not too excited about my state. "I was a little scared that night," she says. "I said, 'Are you okay to follow me up the stairs? You okay?' And you were just, 'Huh-hun-hun.' Ahhh! It's a horror movie for real! All I was worried about was just not to have you trip at me with the chain saw in your hand."

Tobe called "Action!" and it was time to do some cutting. I started on the door. The saw went through the wood easily—those teeth were sharp. When a small chunk of door fell away, I could see Daniel and the camera on the floor inside. I moved to the right a bit to give him a good view of me through the opening. I was pleased that I had enough presence of mind to do that. But I was still concentrating on remembering everything I had to do. I cut some more, including inadvertently sawing into the door frame. (Later the owners would not be happy about that.) Then I kicked the door in and stepped through.

Daniel jumped up and ran out. He left the camera on the floor, still running.

In that moment, I forgot what I was supposed to do next. I paused and watched him run out of the room. Then I remembered and jumped to it—I turned and ran up the stairs.

Daniel says he was not stoned. "Somehow I didn't know the marijuana brownies were around," he says. "But all I remember was a lot of the crew was, like, laughing and giggling and lying around. I just kept on shooting."

We got the shot, though it looks a little goofy now. Leatherface does a dopey, exaggerated double take before he turns and heads up the stairs after Sally. By now Sally has already run into a small room where Grandpa and a very dead, desiccated Grandma sit. Grandpa is supposed to look dead, too—only later do we realize that he is not. Grandma is not even in the script. Bob Burns added her just to show that there had been women in the family at some time.

Sally retreats to the landing and starts back down, till she realizes that she is trapped: Leatherface is lumbering up the stairs, closing the distance. She backtracks and dives out the window. This last bit on the stairs was the part Marilyn was worried about. I came up them after her, but for once she was faster than I was, maybe because of her fear and my befuddlement. She was well ahead of me and headed to the window by the time I reached the landing.

Of course, Marilyn was not going to do the jump herself. Script supervisor Mary Church would instead. Without an actual professional stunt double, Mary had to take the fall for Marilyn a couple of times. "I think the reason I did stunts was because, one, I was game and, two, I fit into Marilyn's clothes," Mary says.

The trouble was that Mary was stoned, too. "I had no clue, and I thought Sally was a really good cook and scarfed down some brownies, and I wasn't feeling any pain. It's like, 'You want me to jump off a roof?' I thought that was brilliant. I remember Ron Bozman getting so pissed when he found out."

The crew set up a mattress nested against some wood scaffolding at the roof edge, about six feet out from the window and four feet below it. Mary, blonde wig and all, would dive out the window and onto the mattress.

"You kind of forget the adrenaline factor," Mary says, "and so I burst out of the window, and I just barely caught the end lip of the mattress, and I nearly sailed off the damn thing, but I did catch the lip of it."

"I remember that she almost missed it," Larry says. "There was a heart-stopping moment there because the way she came out, she was in no position to take a fall safely from that distance."

"Not to be stupid about it," Mary says, "but it didn't occur to me I'd get hurt. Just didn't occur to me. And so maybe stunt people think, *Well, I'm going to be careful, and I'm just not going to get hurt.*"

Mary was lucky that time. It would have been a long fall.

As Marilyn found out.

Marilyn had to complete Sally's fall from the second floor so the camera would see her hit the ground. But instead of having her jump from the back porch and land in the dirt—a fall of about four feet—Tobe had her dropped from the roof. The ceilings were high in that old house, maybe ten feet, making the roof about fourteen feet up from the ground. Two crewmembers held her by her arms and dangled her off the edge of roof, so she still had a fall of about eight feet. And she landed hard.

"I think I do remember something like that," Marilyn says, "but I blocked that all these years, because that's ridiculous. That was stupid. Then I had to run. Oh dear, I do remember that."

"How did we get away with it?" Ron says. "She could have broken something, and we'd have been out of business. I mean, it's like God protects fools."

———•———

We were now into the second part of the chase, which would end when Sally reached the gas station.

In an interview in *Village Voice*, Tobe mentioned Marilyn's injuries at this stage of the chase. "Marilyn had busted both knees up, she was bleeding badly, she was . . . pretty badly injured," he said. "It was terrible, but it played very well."

Here the audience does see Marilyn and me in the same frame. Sally is running directly toward the camera, with Leatherface close behind. It looks like I could have reached out with the saw and touched her—and I probably could have. Clearly Marilyn is running hard—she is barreling along. I, on the other hand, am not—I am jogging along behind her. Any faster and I would have run over her.

From Franklin's death to Sally's arrival into the Cook's open arms at the gas station, the chase lasts about five and a half minutes. But, with its edge-of-your seat tension and Sally's terror in the face of Leatherface's relentless pursuit, it feels like an eternity on-screen. And filming the chase felt like an eternity, too. According to the shooting schedule, only a night and a half were allotted for shooting it, but it felt like—and had to have been longer than that by—several days, especially considering the brownies.

"Would I have done it again?" Marilyn asks. "'Okay, Marilyn, let's do another take with you and Gunnar. Go ahead, Gunnar, chase her with the chain saw.' Today I would have said, 'Are you out of your mind?' To this day, the stupidest thing was having you chase me with the chain saw in the middle of the night, or up the stairs, or all through the woods and all down through the valley. Because we were crazy."

And from here it only got worse for Sally. And for Marilyn.

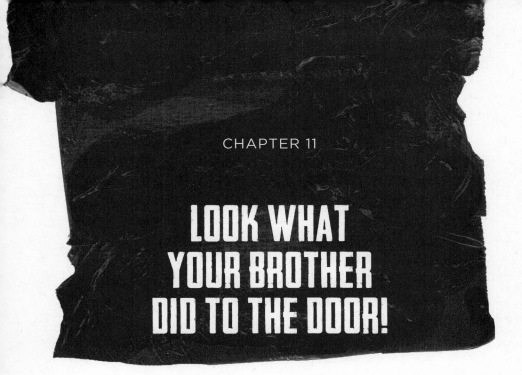

CHAPTER 11

LOOK WHAT YOUR BROTHER DID TO THE DOOR!

I had one more bit of business to shoot once Sally reached the gas station and escaped Leatherface. Tobe wanted Leatherface to have a tantrum at the edge of the building, as if angry that he could not come around to the front and continue his chase. So I stomped around for the camera in a lame attempt to express Leatherface's feelings. And then I was done. (Luckily for me, that footage was never used.)

The shooting continued that night: we still had several hours of darkness and would be shooting Sally's encounter with the Cook. Now free of my mask and chain saw, I decided to hang around a while to watch. I had seen only a bit of Jim Siedow's acting in the early gas station scene and wanted to see more of him in action.

Jim did not beat Marilyn unconscious right away. Sally has burst through the gas station door, where the kindly gas station guy, played by Jim, calms her down. Then he shuffles off to get his truck. This is Sally's moment, a close-up to show her horror after everything that has happened—the disappearance of her friends, Franklin's brutal death, and Leatherface's pursuit. She is in shock and slowly becomes aware of her surroundings, including the red-lit sausages hanging in a nearby cooker. Marilyn needed to convey all that in her close-up.

Tobe called "Action!" and Marilyn started. But he let the camera run, forcing Marilyn to continue well beyond the eighteen or twenty seconds of footage he would actually use.

"We had a fresh load of film which would run eleven minutes before you had to reload," Daniel Pearl says. "And we shot the entire eleven minutes. I'm thinking to myself the whole time, *When is this going to end? When is he going to say 'Cut!?'* Well, eventually we rolled out, which I could hear. I looked at Tobe, and he was just standing there, completely dumbfounded in amazement: 'What on earth am I looking at?'"

"I do remember staring at the sausage a long time," Marilyn says, "but I was told, 'Action!' and I never heard 'Cut!' I'm just doing my thing. I give him credit for letting the actor go as far as she could go. That's a sign that he trusted me maybe, or didn't trust me—I can't figure it. If he didn't trust me, he let me have all this time so he'd get the right shot. Or I was just so perfect that, God, he had eleven minutes of Academy Award material, and he didn't know what to pick. But I kind of think it was eleven minutes to make sure we got the shot. 'Give the blonde eleven minutes.'"

It was an odd bit of stillness in the middle of this hectic shooting in which the tone otherwise seemed to be "Okay, let's do it again."

And then came the beating. The gas station guy—we come to know him as the Cook—returns with his truck. But now he is carrying a sack, a rope, and a knife. Somehow these clues alert Sally that something bad is about to happen.

A struggle begins. The Cook is supposed to beat Sally with the broom till she is subdued, then tie her up and stuff her into the bag. But the beating did not look convincing, likely because the broom was fake—a lightweight shaft with a broom head. The blows seemed to have no weight.

According to Ted Nicolaou there was some discussion that the scene had to be more violent, after which they switched to the real broom. But even so, sweet-tempered Jim just could not bring himself to hit Marilyn hard. So he held back every time he hit her.

"We kept doing take after take after take," Marilyn says. "And finally Tobe goes, 'Jim, Jim, you've got to hit the girl. You look like you're pulling every shot.' Jim said to Tobe, 'I am, I am. I don't want to hit the girl.' Then everybody's bitching. 'We're losing our light, we're losing our sound. We're hearing noise now. Two trucks coming down the highway. Look, the sun's coming up. They're all going to be here in just a minute to open up the gas station. We can't afford this place.' Everybody's bickering and yelling and screaming, and everybody's thinking, *What are we going to do? We're running out of money.*

"And I finally said, 'Jim, just hit me.' And he goes, 'I can't hit you.' 'Jim just hit me, or we're never going to get through this.' So on that take he smacked me so good I went down, and fainted, and got a black eye. Now we had to look at my black eye and fix my cheekbone for continuity every time. But it looked real.

"I liked Jim a lot, even though I'm supposed to hate him," she says. "The man was an actor. But he had a lot of integrity. He worried about the young girl he's playing off of, whereas some other male actors I knew didn't do that. Jim, he would be all caught up in the moment, scaring me to death and really scaring me with the broom. All I'm seeing is this angry madman coming at me with the broom. I'm frightened as hell. Then afterwards he would say, 'Are you okay?'"

Tobe once said that they shot seventeen takes of that beating before he had what he wanted.

Marilyn had had enough. "I got out of there that night and I got to go home," she says. "Jim was just so sad. He kept saying, 'Oh, my Lord, I'm sorry, Marilyn. Let me see your face. Are you okay?' It was so terrible, but it was dawn by then, and all we cared about was just getting out of there."

When shooting resumed the next night, it was time for the Cook to toss the bagged Sally into the truck and take her to meet the family. Marilyn did not want to do it. "There's no reason for me to sit in the bag and have this madman go 'Hee-hee-hee,'" she says. "And have Tobe and Kim tittering and teetering and hee-hawing on the side, which they do. I thought, *Uh-uh, that's where I want my double.*" So Mary Church got into the bag.

This scene really reveals the duality of the Cook's personality—and Jim's acting ability. As soon as he dumps Sally into the truck, the Cook hops out to take care of his responsibilities. "Had to lock up and get the lights," he says when he gets back in, as if Sally might care. "The cost of electricity is enough to drive a man out of business."

Then, after this spell of normalcy, the Cook regresses to crazy as he pokes Sally with the broom handle. It is a sick pleasure. The look in the Cook's face is as if he is sneaking a peak at a sex show. Then he pokes her again. He is getting off on this, but his sexual stimulation is in the brutality.

The script shows what Tobe and Kim wanted Jim to portray in the Cook: "He seems to enjoy torturing her and, at the same time, to be afraid that the torture will produce some terrible reaction with which he will be unable to cope." Tobe said in a later commentary that the Cook has this running conflict because he is not sure where the moral line is drawn.

The Cook has a demonic element in him, but he is afraid of it and keeps trying to push it away. Seen another way, he acts like there's order in the world, but then he gives in to the chaos within himself. The kindly uncle unleashes his overpowering desire to kill, all the while pretending it is distasteful. Though he seems normal from a distance, he becomes more horrific the closer we get.

Jim was the only one who could have pulled it off. He was the best actor among us. "When the camera turned on, he was ready to go," Ed Neal says. "When you needed to get a little crazier he would. And then when he needed to be not so crazy, like when he's in the store scene with Marilyn, here's this psychotic man talking about this horrible thing, but in a very low-keyed, laid-back kind of way, which is scarier than anything."

John Landis says that this is one of the scenes in *Chain Saw* that stand out for him. "That was very disturbing to me because it's relentless," he says. "I mean, these guys are insane—just the glee and the sheer sadism of it."

It got worse.

As the Cook approaches the house, he spots the Hitchhiker. The two have a little encounter in front of the truck in which the Cook beats the Hitchhiker with his broom handle. It is a beautiful bit of film, the rising dust glowing from the headlights as the two silhouetted men dance and shuffle. It looks quite real. In fact it is real. Jim was actually beating Ed.

To light the shot, Daniel put two 1000-watt lights on the truck's bumper to simulate its headlights and illuminate the rising dust. He got the idea, he says, from watching a car driving behind another, with dust being kicked up into the headlights. He liked the way the light hit that dust, and he wanted to duplicate the feel.

Ed and Jim worked out the choreography. "The trick, because Jim was so much shorter than I was, was not to stand up," Ed says. "So I crouched down as low as I could get to make Jim appear to be taller. Another thing that really helped was he was actually really hitting me with an oak dowel rather than a balsa wood one."

With a bigger budget, Ed says, "there would have been a stick wrangler who would have had balsa wood or Featherlite or plastic or something painted to look like a stick. But here they were, just, 'Oh, here, use this.' So poor Jim is smacking me about, about to break my bones with this thing. He didn't have a clue that it was hurting as much as it was. A lot of the scene is played, and you see me cowering and jumping and leaping like a scalded gnome out of the way. It was in real time because it was really hurting." I think Marilyn would understand.

Of course, if the Cook was worried about the electrical bill, he is really not going to be happy about the sliced-up door, screaming to the Hitchhiker, "Look what your brother did to the door!" It is another curious juxtaposition for the Cook, worried about appearances, the dollar value, and the cost of repairing the door, while seemingly indifferent to the value of Sally's life.

Leatherface comes tottering out from behind the metal door. He has been in the kitchen, apparently making dinner. He is now in a completely different mode. The aggressive, chain-saw-wielding killer is gone. His manner has changed. He moves differently and cowers. He now wears a different mask, that of an old lady with gray hair tied up in a bun. He also has on a large, frilly apron and carries a wooden spoon. He has been domesticated. The mask is the key. It reflects—or maybe constitutes—who he is right now. And right now Leatherface is some kind of grandmother, a homebody getting dinner ready for her family. (Maybe she has baked some cornbread to go with those sausages.) This introduces a bit of sexual ambivalence, or at least duality, in Leatherface, which becomes more apparent when we get to the dinner scene.

The Cook berates Leatherface for the door, and then wants to know what happened to "them other kids." The terrified Leatherface is desperate to reassure him. Bent down in subservience, he backs away, moving around the kitchen squawking and squealing and patting different objects—the freezer, the butcher's table, Franklin's wheelchair. It's bizarrely funny to see this massive man with a voice like the squawk of a parrot.

Originally, Leatherface had some lines in this scene—not that they were intelligible. But they were written out. His first line is, "A ab e y ob er wew ober." Then, after a few moments he says, "Ibe goba igee em a."

Though seeming gibberish, the lines were actually supposed to mean something, as Tobe explained to me. According to what I wrote in my script, the first line meant roughly, "How are you?

Welcome home. Supper's almost ready." The next line meant, "I've been a good boy and I got 'em all." There were some more lines over the next couple of minutes—they all pretty much went the same way. (My favorite line, intended as a "hello-how-are-you-sit-here" greeting to Grandpa when Leatherface brings some cold cuts from the kitchen, was "Aba de ah du o day; erik beaka obida tey." Pure poetry, echoing Stephen Foster and the Beatles.

Tobe wanted me to deliver these lines as if Leatherface knew what he was trying to say but could not quite get his mouth to work right. Thus, "Ibe goba igee em a" could, with a stretch of the imagination, sound a bit like, "I've been a good boy and I got 'em all." The rhythm is sort of there.

So I did it that way on the first take. Tobe called "Cut!" Nope, he said, it did not work. The problem was that there was too much intelligence in Leatherface if he merely had trouble getting the words to come out right. I agree—my sense of him was that he was so empty that he really could not speak.

So Tobe told me to do it again. This time I should think of Leatherface as knowing that these sounds we make mean something—after all, he understands what his brothers tell him—but he does not know how to form a thought and turn that thought into words, intelligible or not.

I tried it that way, making a series of meaningless squawks and pointing around the room as if Leatherface actually thought he was saying something. It worked, and we stuck with that for the rest of Leatherface's lines. Some we dropped entirely, since they were pointless. My favorite line "interpretation" was when Leatherface is defending himself from the Cook and his raised broomstick. The line was written, "I iba i i iba i," meaning "yes." I said, "*Ibe!*" It was high-pitched and thin, and summed it all up for me. I still say it now and then, usually when I'm taking a walk in the woods and think of Leatherface for no reason.

Kim and Tobe clearly intended the black humor that is embedded in this and other scenes. As Kim said about writing the script, he knew he had a scene right if it made Tobe laugh. For Tobe, this strange humor was a way to get to the insanity of the characters.

A writer named George Lellis was on set the night we filmed these scenes. In his subsequent article for the Austin magazine *A.P.T.*, he described the process of shooting one particular piece: The Hitchhiker was to run from the kitchen to the stairs, with the dollying camera following him from the dining room into the hall. Then the camera was to turn and dolly back into the dining room, where the Cook was trying to quiet Sally—all in one smooth shot. His description explains why filming was so slow.

"Hooper was adamant about getting the movements between actors and camera perfectly synchronized," Lellis wrote. "'It's pointless to do it so complexly if we're going to have to cut it up,' he said. The camera's trucking back and forth, plus the pan to and away from the moving figure running up the stairs, was rehearsed and made smooth in itself, then rehearsed with the actors. This made for, I was told, one of the shooting's slowest nights, but I was amazed at the carbon-copy uniformity of performance that the actors seemed to produce in each rehearsal and take."

Of course, sometimes our performances were not so carbon-copy perfect, as we would see immediately afterward. (George Lellis was still there, as I recall, yet he did not report on this.) Once the Cook has calmed down and Leatherface is back to preparing dinner, the Hitchhiker calls down from the upstairs landing, "Hey, Leatherface, gimme a hand with Grandpa!" Leatherface obliges, of course, and trots up the stairs.

Getting Grandpa down the stairs was a challenge. Facing him, I lifted the front of his chair and backed down the steps as Ed held its back. But John Dugan, playing Grandpa, started muttering under his breath, as if he were trying to be funny. The distraction made me lower the chair front slightly—just enough so that John, now completely limp, slid out of the chair, between my feet, and onto the steps.

So Ed and I hauled the chair back up and John settled back into it for the ride down. Once again he started muttering and then slid out of the chair. We did this a couple more times. I was convinced that he assumed that his heavy makeup would keep him safe from any repercussions. Finally, as he settled in for another trip down the stairs, I leaned forward and muttered to him. I don't remember exactly what I said, but it was something like, "Do that again and I will rip your head off. Slowly." Whatever my exact words, this time John stayed in place.

When I ask John about it years later, he says he was just following Tobe's instructions. "He wanted me completely limp, like I didn't have a bone in my body, thoroughly relaxed," John says. "You guys couldn't keep that chair level, so I just slid out, and nobody cut."

This scene was John's first day in makeup. Dottie Pearl labored over him in the un–air-conditioned van for seven or eight hours getting the prosthetic makeup applied. And from there John would go into the already overly hot house, with no air moving and its windows covered. The sweat is visible on Marilyn's face—that is not a spritz from makeup.

"That was miserable," John says. "Just the perspiration underneath the mask. It's like when you're trick-or-treating as a child, when you're between houses you always lift that mask up because it's so hot inside. I didn't have the option to do that. It was glued down to my face and you could feel the sweat running down. It was itchy and hot. It was a drag. So I had to go kind of Zen." I wish I had thought of the Zen thing myself.

John knew that portraying Grandpa would be a challenge. "I thought this is going to be difficult because he doesn't say anything," John says. "How do you pull this off without uttering a word? I'm a theater person used to memorizing reams of dialogue, and here's this part which is a pretty major role, and he doesn't say anything."

I know what he means.

———·———

When Leatherface and the Hitchhiker bring Grandpa downstairs, they decide to feed him Sally's blood. Leatherface grabs a bone-handled knife from the dining table and slices her finger, which he then sticks into Grandpa's mouth. The old man works on it like a suckling baby.

Tobe told John that Grandpa "was an embryonic old man," John says. "He's so old that he's become an infant, almost an embryo. Even the feeding on Sally's finger, Kim talked to me about it. He said, 'Have you ever seen a baby when they nurse? How their hands and their legs start going?' So I knew exactly what he was talking about." And that is exactly what he did. It was disturbingly creepy.

It is actually much creepier.

We were having problems with the prop knife. To make it look like Leatherface had actually cut Sally, Bob Burns had taped a tube to the side of the blade away from the camera. The tube led from a bulb of fake blood in my hand to the tip of the blade. The blade, in turn, was covered with a piece of clear adhesive tape, so it had no edge to actually cut Marilyn. As I slashed the knife along her fingertip, I was to squeeze the bulb and deposit the fake blood on her finger.

But no blood came out. Bob fiddled with the knife. He handed it back to me, saying it was fixed. We shot again—nothing. He fixed it again. It did not work. I do not know how many more takes we shot—maybe five, maybe six. I was getting frustrated. The heat and long hours were getting to me. The knife failed again. This time, when Bob handed the "fixed" knife back to me, I decided to make sure it worked. I turned away from the others and quickly stripped the protective tape off the blade. I tested the blade with my thumb—nice and sharp.

I would cut her for real. I wanted to be done with this shot, whatever the damage.

The camera rolled, I grabbed Marilyn's finger, sliced quickly with the knife, and watched the blood ooze out. I squeezed her finger a bit to get more blood, then stuck it into John's mouth. He went into infant mode and sucked it down, not knowing that the blood was real.

As he watched, Ed thought, *God, that looks great.*

Marilyn did not know I had cut her on purpose. In fact, no one else knew I had even cut her. (Well, whoever bandaged her finger must have known.) Marilyn did not find out till many years later, when we were answering questions at a *Chain Saw* screening, and I mentioned casually what had happened.

She was stunned and upset. "All these years I've been telling people that it's an accidental thing with the prop knife," she says. "Then you're on stage with me and you go, 'Oh, come on, Marilyn, we really had to cut you, we were running out of time, and the knife wouldn't work.' I was shocked, I was angry, I was mad, I was furious. I couldn't believe it, I thought, 'You're kidding. He's not for real. Yes, he is. They couldn't be that cruel.'"

Actually, I was the only one being cruel that time. And it wasn't so much that we were running out of time. I was just running out of patience. Luckily, Marilyn has since forgiven me.

John, too, was quite surprised when he found out, though his reaction was a little different. "I didn't find out until years later I was actually sucking on her blood, which is kind of erotic really," he says. "I do recall some sexual stirrings during that scene. Although it was playacting, it was still . . . to have this woman under our control and her screaming, she's beautiful and we're doing weird shit to her. There's some primal thing that comes alive. I hate to admit that."

By that time everyone was getting a bit primal. I certainly was.

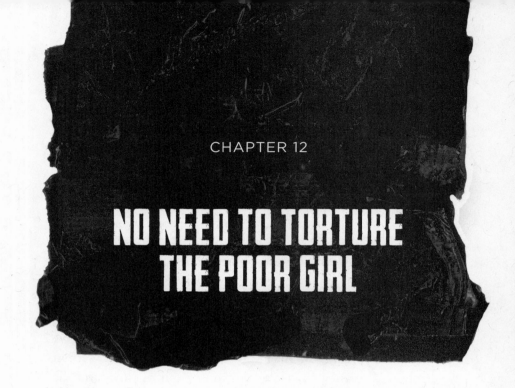

CHAPTER 12

NO NEED TO TORTURE THE POOR GIRL

Finally, we started filming the dinner itself (known by cast and crew as "the last supper"). Sally opens her eyes after having fainted while Grandpa was sucking her blood. She sees a series of dead objects on the table, including a chicken with its eyes sewn shut. She spots Grandpa, puckering his mouth as if still savoring her blood, and she starts screaming. Now we see all of the family arranged around the table—the Hitchhiker, the Cook, Grandpa, and Leatherface—all howling along with her screams of terror in pure joy.

The Cook interrupts the howling with "Quiet!" He clearly is enjoying himself, but once again he pulls back, fearful of his madness, saying, "It can't be helped, young lady." His outburst frightens Leatherface, who hangs his head and plays with the sausage and headcheese on his plate, then gets up and starts to feed Grandpa some headcheese.

Leatherface now wears a third face, transforming him into the Pretty Woman. Once again he uses the mask to represent his state of mind at this moment. He also wears a suit coat to dress up for dinner, maybe because they have a guest. And, lacking women in the household, he again takes on that role, not as a grandmother preparing dinner but as a host in all his—or her—finery.

He is still menacing, though. He and the Hitchhiker work their way down the table toward Sally. The Hitchhiker puts his hand on her face, sticking a finger into her open mouth for a second, while Leatherface reaches out and starts playing with her hair.

The Hitchhiker asks, "You like that face?" In the film Leatherface says nothing, but in the script he says, "Un va uhn," curiously like the old 1950s jazz hipster's "Va, va, voom!" My script margin notes indicated the meaning to be "I like it," but this line and the rest in the scene were cut—after Tobe's earlier change in line readings, there was no point in having Leatherface try to speak again beyond occasional squawks.

"You scared me to death," Marilyn says of my approach. "I didn't know you really at all, and by this time you're not sure if it's real or a movie. And snuff films were just coming at this time and I'm thinking—I'm not in a snuff movie, but I'm thinking *this is too real.* The leering, leering when all you started coming at me, that was really scary. We kept doing, 'Okay, let's [shoot] it from his angle, from Gunnar's, from Ed's, from Jim's, from Grandpa's.'"

There is an undertone of sexual menace in the pair's approach, but nothing happens. After toying with her, they retreat. Clearly, though, Leatherface likes what he sees.

Leatherface's sexual ambiguity was originally carried further in the filming, in a scene edited out before the movie's release. In the script, almost immediately after this, Leatherface wanders into the living room while "tittering and babbling to himself" (as I wrote in my script), making sounds that were supposed to say "You're so pretty!"

Leatherface shambles over to a bucket of faces hanging from the ceiling. He grabs one and looks at it. Its blonde hair looks to be cut in a pageboy. He picks up a small hand mirror and compares the new mask to his current one, deciding which looks better. He rejects the new one, tossing it over his shoulder. (It is obvious in looking at this footage how hard it was for me to see out of the mask. When I looked down to pick up the mirror, I had to tilt my head straight down to see it.) Leatherface bends down again and picks up some face powder. He powders his face grotesquely, the powder flying everywhere in a caricature of some feminine cliché of an earlier time. Then he applies fresh lipstick, doing it with some delicacy, as if sometime in the past he watched his mother putting on her lipstick. Then, checking out his spruce-up in his mirror, he cocks his head to the side, as if admiring what he sees before he returns to the dining room.

I do not think Leatherface is really trying to look feminine in this scene—nor did I back then. After all, he is wearing a suit, not a dress. But he wants to look attractive to Sally. His gender is irrelevant here, as if he really has no sexual identity. But he is smitten by their prisoner.

I can guess why this scene was not used in the movie: Though it would have helped define Leatherface's personality, it is also a dead stop. It would have killed the dinner scene's pacing. The rest of it likely would never have regained its momentum and would have limped to a finish.

Doug Bradley has an interesting take on this deleted scene. "It's a picture of a dressing room, makes Leatherface an actor, makes this a performance," he says. "*Persona* is the Latin word for 'mask' and the word for 'personality.' Persona is what we present to the world. It's something that we do all the time, we put on our 'masks.' I think that would have been a great element to put in for Leatherface. He's aware that this is a performance." Exactly. And for Leatherface, his persona is literally in his mask.

As the scene wears on, Sally's screams intensify until she pleads, "I'll do anything you want."

"At that time in my life, I thought that was the dirtiest thing you could say," Marilyn says. "It was pretty damn serious. Nowadays it comes out of everybody's mouth. Now they're doing it for free, they're jumping for it. But in those days, 'I'll do anything you want': you just didn't say that. You never said that."

But, as Marilyn says of Sally's tormentors, "Nobody gets it." They do not react at all. But then, this is not the kind of offer they want. Their sexuality is so repressed that it manifests itself only as sadistic cruelty. Their excitement is in watching her suffer, and they are already getting off on that. This makes them even more horrifying.

The sadism in *Chain Saw* extends beyond this scene. "There is a certain joy in people being hurt," Bill Vail says, "which was encouraged when we were shooting the film. And things that happened out of happenstance a number of times with me and Pam were the takes that were kept, where we would hurt ourselves just in the course of shooting the movie. We were coming down, Pam and I are coming down the little hill down to where we think the swimming hole is, and I tripped and twisted my ankle, Bill Vail did. It is still in the film. That was one of those instances that I was talking about where someone hurt themselves in the course of making the movie, that's the take we used. Tobe liked that."

Think, too, of Teri's suffering as Pam.

"Of course," Marilyn says. "'Hit her harder! Let her fall more!' Yes, it was 'the funnier the better.' You could hear Tobe and Kim cackling all the time. They would find it so funny that I'm sitting there dying. Then, of course, that would just make me feel worse, and really make me feel like crying, it really made me feel small. Then they'd be going 'tee-hee' more because now I'm crying. Oh yeah, they did that on everybody."

"I started thinking about just the simple fact of the abuse of the main character," Bill says, "and the torture she was put through, and the abuse she was put through. Because in a way you could look at it as a porno, and that people who get off on the pain and torture of other people could see that this movie is like a movie to get off on, something you'd watch in your bedroom without anybody else around."

Though the camera does not linger on death but just moves on as if death and its details are not important, that is not the case with Sally's torture. Nowhere is this more obvious than when the camera moves in on Marilyn's eyes in the dinner scene. Sally is in a frenzy of fear, and the camera stays tight on her, closing in, lingering on the details of her bloodshot eyes.

Marilyn's treatment when they shot that close-up was no different from Sally's misery. It was shot later, when principal photography had finished and the editing had started.

Tobe asked Marilyn down to the Shoot Out offices, where Daniel Pearl, Ted Nicolaou, and Larry Carroll were based. "Tobe just said, 'Marilyn, do you want to come to the studio and see what's going on?'" Marilyn says. "And he goes, 'I just want a few shots of your eyes.' And so I went down there, and it seemed like four to five hours. I wasn't able to check my eyes, the camera was just on them. I don't realize that after I cried so much and the camera is on them, all this stuff is floating in my eye, and it's getting redder and redder and grosser and grosser. Of course, they don't say, 'Oh Marilyn, let's take a moment.' They thought, 'This is getting better. Give her another couple hours and her eyes will really look crappy.' Then they kept it on, kept it on. They're not going to say, 'Are you okay? Did you hurt yourself? Are you uncomfortable?' They're not going to do that."

Larry was there for the shooting. "I remember poor Marilyn when we did the close-ups on her in the chair," he says. "I don't know how long that poor girl was screaming over and over and over again. Then finally Tobe had what he wanted, and everybody left. Marilyn is there, just the two of us, and she's just devastated. However long it was, like everything else, it was horribly long in that film. I think actually I wanted to drive her home that night because she was just . . . there was nothing left. I think for Tobe, the performance that he wanted, about the only way that he knew how to get it out of her was basically torturing her, and he did. It was horrific."

Art director Bob Burns at home, surrounded by *Chain Saw* props.

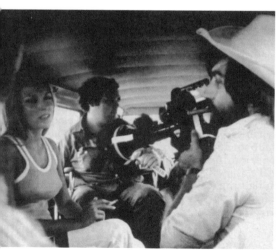

TOP: Bill Vail (Kirk), Terry McMinn (Pam), and director Tobe Hooper prepare for a scene at the van.

BOTTOM LEFT: Tobe Hooper (RIGHT) does a camera test on Marilyn Burns (Sally) in the van, with Paul Partain (Franklin) in the background.

BOTTOM RIGHT: With Gunnar (LEFT) looking on, Tobe Hooper sets up Leatherface's fall and chain saw injury.

OPPOSITE, TOP: Tobe Hooper discusses a scene at the old Franklin place with (LEFT TO RIGHT) cinematographer Daniel Pearl, Allen Danziger (Jerry), Marilyn Burns, and Bill Vail.

OPPOSITE, BOTTOM: At the gas station, Tobe Hooper (LEFT) directs Jim Siedow (Cook) with Marilyn Burns and Daniel Pearl in the background. Gunnar is partly visible behind Marilyn.

OPPOSITE, TOP: Our ill-fated travelers: (LEFT TO RIGHT) Kirk (Bill Vail), Pam (Teri McMinn), Jerry (Allen Danziger), Sally (Marilyn Burns), and Franklin (Paul Partain).

OPPOSITE, BOTTOM: Pam (Teri McMinn) approaches the house.

ABOVE: Leatherface carries Pam (Teri McMinn) to her fate.

All dressed up, Leatherface enjoys a bit of dinner table banter.

The only picture of Gunnar unmasked from the filming.

ABOVE: Producer Ron Bozman at the table during the dinner scene filming, with assistant camera-man Lou Perryman (LEFT) and sometime camera operator Lynn Lockwood (RIGHT) behind him.

OPPOSITE, TOP LEFT: An exhausted Marilyn Burns, with Lou Perryman behind her, during a shot set up for the dinner scene.

OPPOSITE, TOP RIGHT: Wayne Bell on microphone during the dinner scene.

OPPOSITE, BOTTOM: Lynn Lockwood and Marilyn Burns setting up for a shot at the dinner table.

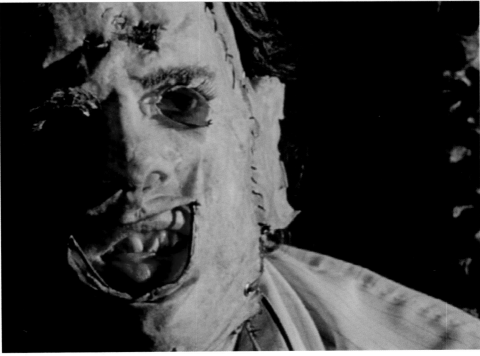

OPPOSITE: Leatherface feeds Grandpa (John Dugan) some of Marilyn Burns's real blood.

TOP: Leatherface runs from the house.

BOTTOM: Leatherface and his baby teeth as he contemplates his victims.

Who will survive
and what will be left of them?

America's most bizarre and brutal crimes!...

'THE TEXAS CHAINSAW MASSACRE"

What happened is true. Now the motion picture that's just as real.

THE TEXAS CHAIN SAW MASSACRE · A Film by TOBE HOOPER · Starring MARILYN BURNS, PAUL A. PARTAIN, EDWIN NEAL, JIM SIEDOW and GUNNAR HANSEN as "Leatherface"
Production Manager, RONALD BOZMAN · Music Score by TOBE HOOPER and WAYNE BELL · Music Performed by ARKEY BLUE, ROGER BARTLETT & FRIENDS, TIMBERLINE ROSE,
LOS CYCLONES · Story & Screenplay by KIM HENKEL and TOBE HOOPER · Producer / Director, TOBE HOOPER · COLOR · A BRYANSTON PICTURES RELEASE.

R RESTRICTED

OPPOSITE: The original 1974 Bryanston poster.

TOP LEFT: Japanese *Chain Saw* poster.

TOP RIGHT: The French poster announces "Massacre of the Chain Saw" "After 5 years of prohibition."

BOTTOM LEFT: The Spanish poster for "The Massacre from Texas."

ABOVE: The German poster for "Blood Judgement in Texas."

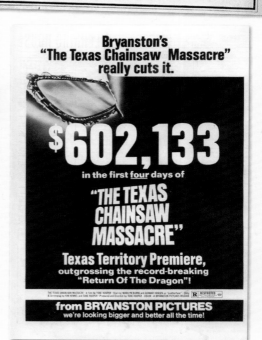

TOP LEFT: An ad mat used for newspaper promotion.

TOP RIGHT: Exploiting *Chain Saw*'s MoMA and Cannes connections for a 1975 New York City run.

BOTTOM LEFT: A London ad for the original release of *The Texas Chain Saw Massacre*.

BOTTOM RIGHT: Bryanston's *Variety* ad announcing *Chain Saw*'s gross sales its first four days.

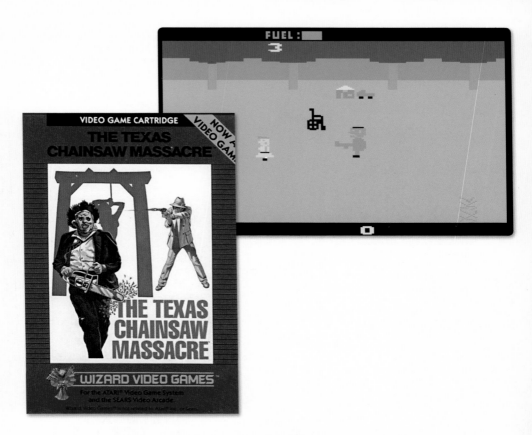

TOP: A screen shot from Wizard Video's *The Texas Chainsaw Massacre* game.

MIDDLE: Wizard Video's *The Texas Chainsaw Massacre* game, advertised as "the first violent video game."

BOTTOM: NECA's *The Texas Chainsaw Massacre* lunch box.

The *Chain Saw* family take a moment on the porch.
CLOCKWISE FROM TOP LEFT: Grandma, Grandpa
(John Dugan), the Cook (Jim Siedow), Leatherface
(Gunnar), and the Hitchhiker (Ed Neal).

Stuart Gordon talked to Bob Burns about the dinner scene. "He talked about you guys working yourselves to exhaustion," Stuart says. "He also talked about Marilyn Burns and that she was really going around the bend on this. The reason her performance is so riveting is that she really was kind of starting to lose it. The hours, the intensity of the scenes that she was doing, and so forth, kind of caught up with her. Well, she's the audience; there's always one person in a movie that they're sort of like the surrogate audience member the audience identifies with, and that's who she was. That's how you felt when you walked out of that movie, that you'd been beaten with a broom."

In fact, in one interview Bob called the entire production "a very abusive shoot."

———•———

Of course, our physical and mental agonies were much less severe than Marilyn's. But there were some that we all shared.

It had been brutally hot throughout the filming, but nothing like in the dinner scene, which Daniel also remembers as the hottest days of our shoot. Though the scene takes place at night, we started shooting during the day and continued right through the night and into the next morning, so we covered the windows with layers of heavy black cloth to keep the light out. This also kept fresh air out and let the heat build up inside.

"I needed a lighting plan that would allow us to move quickly," Daniel says, "including getting these raw, nasty-ass photofloods into the fixtures that are around, 250-watt and 500-watt light bulbs, which also didn't do anything to help the heat in the room, and away we went." My guess is that, assuming the outside temperature to be a hundred degrees when we filmed the dinner scene, it was easily a hundred twenty inside.

"The conditions were horrific," Larry says. "I would come from an air-conditioned office and a good night's sleep and a bath within the last seven or eight hours, and everybody was just suffering incredibly. The heat was intense. The hours. Yet it was an interesting set because I remember only seeing you in makeup. I never saw you without the mask on and the whole outfit, which was pretty heavy clothes for summertime." Yes, they were.

But it was not just the heat. It was also the smell. The set had always smelled like a foul combination of stale sweat and an old barn. But the increased heat made the stench brutal. And that heat quickly started to affect the food on the table and the set dressing itself, the skins, bones, and carcasses getting more and more ripe. "The headcheese itself was rotting under the heat conditions," Daniel says, "So it was quite rancid, to say the least. That stuff only helps."

"That was the cheese and the chicken legs and the chicken heads and the dead dogs that didn't get used," Ted adds. "I mean that was truly like a slaughterhouse atmosphere, that scene."

Yes, dead dogs. Some of the crew had found "a vet who had been throwing carcasses in a pile," Daniel Pearl says. After they had been brought to the set, they ripened up pretty well. Dottie Pearl said once that she had tried to keep the smell and the maggots down by injecting the carcasses with formaldehyde. But that had not gone so well. She once pushed the needle right through a carcass and into her leg, dosing herself with the toxin. I never saw the dogs, which were either props in Grandpa's room or out in the back yard unused. The day after shooting the dinner scene, Ron Bozman and his crew, "just out of our minds at that point," piled the carcasses and poured gasoline on them. But the bodies would not burn. Instead they filled the yard with a "smoking dead dog aroma." So Ron buried the carcasses. "The ground was all limestone and miserable," he says. "It was like punishment for doing such a stupid day." This stupid day, our filming of the dinner scene, lasted twenty-six, twenty-eight, or thirty-six hours, depending on whom you talk to.

The smell got up into my mask. I could never get away from it unless I went outside and took the mask off. But Tobe had set a rule that the mask stayed on me during any break unless it was fifteen minutes or longer. And every break was officially five minutes, even if it lasted an hour.

But when I did get free of the mask and got outside for some air, I could not escape the smell, because I *was* the smell. I was the smelliest, ripest part of the set. I had worn the same clothes for four weeks. None of them were ever washed because we were afraid the cleaners would either lose the wardrobe or it would change color. According to Tobe, Marilyn had already lost part of her costume that way. At least she had replacements.

So, isolated as I was during the filming—as Marilyn says, "Leatherface and I didn't hang out"—by this point I was even more unpopular because of my smell. I was shunned.

The worst of it came when we broke for lunch—in the middle of the night, of course. Dottie Pearl took my mask off, and we all went outside to eat. I got in line, and the person in front of me told me to get out of line, that I stank too much to be anywhere near him.

I could understand how my smell was putting them off their feed. It was making even me sick. I asked Dr. Barnes for some nausea pills. Then I lay down somewhere far away from the others, where I could stare up at the stars and take deep breaths of fresh air.

My smell is what most people remember about the dinner scene. "It was unbelievable," Ted says. "We felt sorry for you, you know." So did I.

I did not understand why we kept shooting instead of just finishing up the next night. As far behind schedule as we were, what would an extra day matter? I thought I knew why—that John Dugan, Grandpa, had refused to sit for yet another lengthy makeup session. This was also Daniel's understanding. "He announced that he was never going through this again," Daniel says, "and that we would have to shoot him out, that he was never going to sit in the chair for eight or nine hours again."

But John denies that. "No, I never said that, never," he says. "Young actor, my first film, I would have done it time and time again to get it right. They were concerned because, I think, they only had enough of the makeup for two days."

So we kept shooting because we did not have a third face for John. And, some years later, Jim Siedow confirmed that he had had to go back to Houston the next day, so we would be losing him.

The real issue, however, was that we had so much to shoot, and in such detail, that we could not move through it quickly. The final edited scene at the table itself is almost six minutes long. Usually, there is only one master shot (the shot that serves as the scene's framework in editing). But Tobe wanted two master shots, one from Grandpa's point of view and one from Marilyn's. Tobe also needed all the closer shots, called inserts. These included the two-shot of the Cook and the Hitchhiker bickering; two-shots of Sally with Leatherface, Sally with the Hitchhiker, and Leatherface with Grandpa; and close-ups of each of the five of us. Counting the master shots, that was about ten different angles.

Fair enough. But instead of shooting the inserts as short pieces, for each of these angles Tobe wanted to film the entire scene from beginning to end. And the shots all had to follow the same timing, supposedly to make cutting it together easier. (As little as I knew about filmmaking at the time, this made no sense to me, and still doesn't.)

So we needed at least ten perfect takes of the entire six-minute dinner table scene. If we assume that the actors were close to flawless and the equipment problems nonexistent, my very conservative guess would be that we still had to shoot two to three takes to get each perfect one. That means that to shoot the dining table section, we would need at least twenty-five or thirty takes. (Ted and Daniel confirm my arithmetic.)

So we shot again and again and again. We were going nowhere—well, somewhere, but very slowly. Wayne Bell, who has worked with Tobe on other films, feels this is his pattern. "I have come to think that Tobe always has to have a twenty-six-hour day in every one of his movies. The only other movie I did with him after that was the sequel, with Dennis Hopper [*The Texas Chainsaw Massacre 2* (1986)]. At the end of that movie, it was July 3rd and we had to be done the next day for July 4th, and we ended going all night and into the morning. That was a twenty-six-hour shoot also. And I've heard from other Tobe shoots that there is always this one marathon shoot that is just excruciating."

"I remember just being tied up," Marilyn says, "being screamed at, having the smell of headcheese and your Leatherface outfit and the room itself, the chicken, all the other decaying meat, the decaying set, the decaying crew."

These conditions put us in a stupor. "Truthfully, a lot of it's real foggy to me, kind of dreamlike," John says. "Does that make any sense?" Yes. I got to the point, myself, where I no longer could see what we were doing. I was just trying to keep alive, to get through this day. I no longer even knew where the camera was.

"This is what's going on for hours," Ed says. "It bred a kind of a hysteria, a kind of an acting hysteria that worked wonderfully well for the film itself. I mean to put yourself into a situation where you're supposed to act tired and you are tired. You're supposed to be maniacal and you are maniacal. You're supposed to be psychotic and you are teetering on psychotic because of lack of sleep and an intensity of emotion that you've been asked to sustain over hours of time."

"It was a pretty tough shoot," Marilyn says, "but do you know what made it good? It made it to the camera. All our misery comes out on the film."

We had to keep moving. We were finished at the dinner table. Leatherface and the boys have worked Sally over pretty well. And then the Cook, filling with guilt during her suffering, says, "No need to torture the poor girl."

"The older brother is schizing out between what he really feels about all this killing, about the way these idiot brothers of his are carrying on, and he's looking back and forth between old Grandpa and the Hitchhiker mocking the girl," Tobe said in his interview with Paolo Zelati. "On the one hand he's getting off on it, and then he becomes ashamed of himself, and he looks back to old Grandpa, and he gets afraid of his own thoughts, and he gets afraid of what old Grandpa is going to think of him; and Grandpa doesn't have enough sense to, he doesn't even know he's there anyway. Then finally he says, 'Let's get on with it, I have to open soon. I have to go down and open the store up and get the pits going, get on with it.'"

It is finally time to kill Sally—an honor the boys want to give to Grandpa and his trusty sledgehammer, an honor at which he fails utterly.

We are back in Stooges mode, three incompetents trying to get the fourth to hold the hammer while we push Sally's head into a bucket.

Marilyn was not happy with the way that went. "I went to the bucket," she says, "and then Grandpa hit me over the head with the other prop that was a piece of steel, a sledgehammer." Bob Burns had taken the hammer's iron head off and replaced it with a foam rubber head, but apparently he left the steel shaft. "That hurt," she adds, "That wasn't fake." Some of the blood in Sally's hair is actually Marilyn's.

"The whole sledgehammer thing," John says, was the hardest for him as an actor. "Getting that right, making it look real, like he was actually trying to hit her but didn't have the strength or dexterity to hold the hammer, and Grandpa's frustration in not being able to do it. He wants to be able to do it, but he fucking can't. That seems like it went on forever. Well, they shot from a couple different angles, and I think there were a couple setups. Then everybody else's growing frustration around me. Ed's 'Hit the bitch! Hit her, Grandpa! Hit the bitch!' And Jim off in the corner jumping up and down. I think we all kind of gelled there."

Yes, because by now we all had gone crazy.

I distinctly remember Ed's saying "Kill her! Kill the bitch!" just before Sally escapes. But it is not in the script. It is also not in the movie. The Cook says "Hit that bitch!" and then the Hitchhiker picks up the line, repeating it over and over while he and Leatherface and Grandpa struggle with killing Sally. But somehow I heard it as "Kill the bitch." And I was certain at the time that as Sally/Marilyn broke free of our grasp, I heard the Hitchhiker/Ed yell "Kill the bitch!" one more time. And that is why I, Leatherface/Gunnar at that moment, said to myself, "Yes. Kill. The. Bitch." as I stepped forward.

I was going to kill her. I had lost any sense of my being in a movie. My transformation was complete. Just for that second I had become Leatherface. I had lost all perspective and succumbed to Method after all. Luckily for Marilyn, stepping forward brought me out of my nightmare, and I again knew that this was a movie and I was not Leatherface and I was not going to kill the bitch.

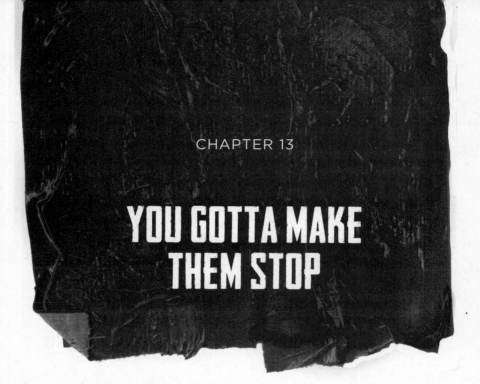

CHAPTER 13

YOU GOTTA MAKE THEM STOP

We finished shooting the dinner scene at dawn, and it would be twenty-four hours before the light was right to resume shooting. I think that this, more than any particular sense of mercy or concern for our mental health, was why we had a day-long break to recover. I do not remember much about that day. I know I went home and took a long shower and slept for most of the day. I remember feeling very clean. I think I talked to my housemate, later, when I got up to make dinner and only then discovered that his girlfriend was living with us. Then I went back to bed to be ready for an early call on set.

This would be our last day of shooting, and we had only about three minutes of movie left to shoot. Sally would jump through the front window, then run down the driveway with the Hitchhiker slashing at her with his straight razor and Leatherface lumbering along behind them. A cattle truck would crush the Hitchhiker, and Leatherface would fall and cut his leg with his saw, allowing Sally time to climb aboard a passing pickup truck. Finally, Leatherface would dance in frustration at her escape. Except for the last bit, all of this takes place at first light, before the sun comes up. Beyond actually shooting in predawn light, we could approximate it only when the sun was behind a cloud (otherwise the light quality would give us away). Waiting between clouds burned much of the day, and we actually filmed Leatherface's dance against the rising sun at sunset.

We started with Sally's dive out the window. Bob Burns and Mary Church had made the breakaway sugar glass, using Karo syrup as a key ingredient. As with Sally's second-floor jump earlier, Mary would perform the stunt, but Marilyn would again have to do the landing. Sally's crash through the glass was shot from inside the house, so Bob and Mary placed empty boxes and a mattress on the ground directly below the window for Mary to land on.

It all took a bit too long to set up, and by the time they shot, the "glass" was starting to dissolve in the humid air. "When I went through it, I was like a glass woman because I had now little particles stuck all over me because the stuff was wet," Mary says. "If they'd waited probably another forty-five minutes, I don't know if there'd been any glass in those windows."

Marilyn was not happy with this arrangement. The actual distance from the window to the ground was only about three feet, and she wanted to do the jump herself. They refused—that was for Mary to do. But for her landing, Marilyn would have to fall from a much higher point, a six-foot scaffolding.

The jump was risky, and this was a bad time to lose our lead actress. She asked to jump instead from the now-broken-out window, but she was again refused. She would have to jump the six feet. "I was really angry," she says. "That's a lot when you're five-foot-two. And it's early in the morning, they have this sugar glass which is crystallized because of the humidity, so when they throw the damn glass on my head, it's in big chunks."

When she landed, Marilyn thought she had broken her ankle. Luckily she had not, but it was very painful. And now she had to run down the driveway.

This also caused a problem for Ed. Hobbled by her ankle, Marilyn was even slower than before. And now Ed had to trail behind without catching her. "So then I came up with the acrobatic, balletic motion of cutting her back and forth," he says, "rather than just jumping on her and grabbing her, which I easily could have done because I was so close." On-screen we see the Hitchhiker close in on Sally quickly, but once he is near, he dances back and forth behind her, arms raised, slashing at her with his razor. I suppose one might call it balletic.

To film Sally and the Hitchhiker running down the driveway and then turning out onto the road, Daniel had his crew set the dolly track at an angle to the driveway, extending out into the road. He could dolly slowly as the two approached and, when they turned, swing the camera and continue to follow them for a distance.

The track blocked part of the road, so we had to close it. We had no permit to shoot on a public road or to stop traffic, so we had to be discreet. We sent a couple of flaggers just over the crest of the hill to stop any traffic while we actually shot. Otherwise they just warned drivers to go slowly. Quick Hill Road was not much traveled, so we almost got away with it.

At one point Ron Bozman stopped a woman while we were filming. "I said, 'Ma'am if you don't mind waiting just a minute, we're filming up here.' She kind of freaked out, and she turned around and drove off. Half an hour later, her husband came driving up with a shotgun in the back. 'You talked to my wife.' I said, 'Sorry, sir, I just asked her to stop for a second.' 'Oh, okay. She got a little hysterical.'"

Soon after that, the sheriff came barreling past the flag crew in his cruiser, over the hill, and right at the dolly. He stopped just a couple of feet short of Daniel and the camera. The famous and feared Sheriff Jim Boutwell got out of his car and said something like, "What are you boys doing?"

"He was very angry," Kim Henkel says.

I was standing nearby, wearing my Pretty Woman mask and holding a smoking chain saw. I did not like the looks of this, and I figured that the sheriff would not either if he got a glimpse of me. So I sidled away to get at least a bush between myself and the sheriff. I set the chain saw down in the tall grass and settled down beside it, my back to the developing drama.

Facing away, I thought I heard the sheriff say something like, "This is my county." I did turn to see Ron—as production manager, our sacrificial lamb—get into the cruiser. He and Sheriff Boutwell sat in there for a long time, and I thought Ron would be going to jail. Then he got out, and the sheriff drove off.

"I was the responsible adult in that situation," Ron says. "I just said, 'We're just doing this. I told you about it.' In truth I probably hadn't talked to him about closing the traffic. Then I just talked my way through it. You just got to go into the belly of the beast and deal with it. He said, 'All right, get out of here as soon as you can.'"

Of course we did just that, which took the rest of the day.

The next sequence to film was the Hitchhiker's death. The Hitchhiker is enjoying himself so much, dancing and slashing behind Sally as they run down the road, that he does not see the approaching cattle truck—a wonderful old Peterbilt semi named "Black Maria." (A fellow named Ed Guinn, who owned it with a friend, drove it in the movie and, in effect, played himself.) The truck smashes into the Hitchhiker and crushes him like a lifeless dummy.

Which it was. Bob had wired a dummy upright in the road for the truck to run over. The dummy does not look great—it's a bit brittle when the truck hits it—but the shot is so quick that the lack of goo hardly matters.

The difficult part of this sequence was getting a close view of the Hitchhiker's death. The long shot showed us the Hitchhiker being crushed, but we needed to see the truck hit him. And we needed to do it without actually running him over.

Daniel knew a way: shoot it in reverse with the camera upside down. When the film was turned right side up, it would play backward. So he mounted the camera upside down in the truck cab, looking down at the Hitchhiker. They rolled film with Hitchhiker Ed pressed against the truck, and then truck driver Ed backed up as fast as he could. Hitchhiker Ed then had to "do the motions of being run over in reverse, so that you just had to do the emotion backwards," he says. "It looks pretty good in the film. It looks pretty realistic."

The sequence was supposed to end with a shot of the dead Hitchhiker's face pasted on the pavement. Ed says it was miserable for him to lie there, cheek against the black asphalt, as they applied blood and then filmed him. He could feel his skin frying.

For me, the experience was more like baking. Some hours into the day's shooting, with the sun high and the heat at its worst, executive producer Jay Parsley found me standing out in the sun in a stupor. I was still holding the saw and still wearing the mask, cooking inside, too befuddled to put the saw down or find some shade.

When Jay got a good look at me, he grabbed the chain saw from my hand and started screaming at Dottie to get herself over here and get my mask off. I do not think that his words were as restrained or as polite as this, though.

Dottie came running, unlaced the mask, and pulled it off. Then Jay led me over to his car. It was a white Buick Riviera with a red leather interior. (Maybe Texans have a weakness for white cars with red leather—that's how John Dugan described Paul Partain's Cadillac, and how I remember the one in that Mexican romance so long ago.) Jay popped the trunk and opened a cooler inside, filled with iced-down Lone Star beers. "Take yourself a couple," he said. I did. Then he led me around to the passenger side and let me in. He started the engine and turned on the air-conditioning full blast.

"We're going for a little ride," he said.

I settled back in the seat, cold air on my face and a cold Lone Star in each fist. I took a long pull on one. *This man is a god,* I thought.

But the good times—and the air-conditioning and beer—could not last. I had a scary shot coming up—Leatherface's encounter with the chain saw when he falls.

It looks straightforward on-screen—the truck driver throws a pipe wrench at Leatherface's head. Leatherface falls and the running saw lands on his leg. But it was going to be hard to pull off. And I was nervous.

Several times during the filming, especially as the day for this stunt approached, I had asked Tobe how we would shoot it. Each time I asked, he would get a thoughtful look and then say, "I don't know. But don't worry, we'll shoot that last." I always felt comforted by his answer—until I realized that he meant that if I were hurt, it would not matter, since by then they would have filmed everything they needed me for. I did not feel so good about that.

Finally, Bob Burns came up with the way to do it. He would tape a piece of sheet metal around my leg, from below my knee to up on my thigh, covering a large area because we could not be sure exactly where the saw would hit me. Then he would tape a steak on top of that—to be the torn, exposed flesh. On top of *that* he would tape a blood bag—to give us a bit of gore.

I agreed to do it.

Tobe then told me that for the close-up of the saw going into my leg, he would have a crew member operate the chain saw. I refused. I would do it myself, I said. It was my leg. He relented.

This seems to be common in low-budget filmmaking, a willingness to take chances to get the shot, reinforced by the lack of money for stunt people. The spirit is commendable, I suppose, but it is mighty risky. In fact, it was downright stupid.

But we did it anyway.

The first part of the shot went fine. Ed Guinn pitched the pipe wrench—one of Bob's balsa marvels—at me, and it banged me square in the forehead. This was a wide shot, so I would have to fall flat on my back on the pavement without a pad to break my fall. Untrained in the fine points of falling, I just let myself fall back, holding my head forward to keep it from slamming into the pavement. It hurt a bit, but I think it looked okay.

Then came the risky part: falling again, this time with the camera closer and with the saw cutting into my leg. Everyone moved in for a close look before we rolled, wondering whether the stunt would work at all—or too well, perhaps. Again there was no pad for me to land on. This time they wanted just to see the end of my fall, so I crouched down with the running saw in my right hand and launched myself back and up so that I would be completely off the ground before I came down. I hit hard. The saw hit my leg. Nothing happened. The toothless chain did not even cut through the pant leg.

We replaced it with the real chain. I crouched again and launched myself. I hit the ground and the saw hit my leg. It cut through the pant leg, blood bag, and steak in an instant.

I felt a stab of pain and jerked the saw away. I clamped my free hand down on the cut. Blood spurted up between my fingers. I stayed frozen for a long moment.

And then the pain went away.

Someone's friend was visiting the set that day. She had stood nearby with the rest of the crew as they watched my fall. The moment was intense. It was silent. And then she yelled out, "Cut! It's a print!"

Tobe, his ever-present cigar in his hand, looked over at her in surprise. Then he nodded. "Yeah, cut," he said. "Print it."

What had happened? The saw had, indeed, cut through the layers covering my leg. But when it hit the sheet metal it went no deeper. Still, it kept grinding—so fast that in a short instant it heated up the metal and burned my leg. I was not cut after all. As for the blood, there had been plenty left in the blood bag. When I clamped my hand on the cut, my grip forced the blood to spurt between my fingers.

Later I would find a small red spot on my leg from the burn. It was gone the next day.

No one bothered to take that rig off my leg after that—maybe because it was late afternoon and we had more to shoot before the sun went down. Still, the sheet metal kept me from bending my knee, and that was the look we needed—with his leg cut that way, Leatherface was going to be gimpy. And slow. (I always thought leaving the steak on there was wasteful, particularly on such a low-budget shoot. Bob should have retrieved the steak for us to grill and dismember in some kind of ersatz cannibal blood ritual. Ted jokes, "We probably did have that for dinner.")

There were two bits left to shoot, Sally's escape in a conveniently arriving pickup truck and Leatherface's frustrated reaction.

Sally makes for the truck. She's hurting. She moves slowly. Leatherface is moving slowly, too. But he is gaining on her.

All Marilyn had to do was climb into the bed of the truck and let the driver (our editor, Larry Carroll) haul out of there before I caught up to her. Tobe told her to struggle to get into the truck, to do it slowly to build the tension.

The first take, Marilyn hobbled up to the truck and got a foot up on the rear tire to lift herself up into the bed. But she was slow, so slow that I caught up with her before she got aboard. So we did it again. She was too slow again. We shot it again, and again, each time struggling with our timing, never quite getting it right.

Finally, Marilyn clambered into the truck, her foot slipping repeatedly on the tire for dramatic effect, as Tobe wanted. She rolled into the truck's bed just as I was arriving. Perfect timing.

But Larry forgot to drive away.

So, never one to ruin a shot, I figured the only thing I could do was to keep going, to climb in after her. I got my left foot up on the back bumper and pulled myself up. Just as I shifted my weight forward and was raising my right foot off the ground, Larry remembered to leave. He took off fast, pitching me back. My right foot landed back on the ground, but my left caught between the bumper and the fender. The truck started to drag me.

I did not see my life flash before my eyes, but I saw my future— I imagined myself being dragged to my death as Marilyn screamed for Larry to stop. And I imagined his amazement at how realistic her screams were.

I rolled violently to the left, which twisted my foot and pulled it clear of the bumper, leaving me quite alive, but a bit shaken. I think I still had the chain saw in my hand.

We did another take, or two, to get it right. (Marilyn would have to come back the next day to reshoot Sally's insane, screaming relief in the back of the truck as it drove away. Marilyn never could catch a break.)

"That we did that film without a stunt coordinator and without all that, and that nobody got really hurt is amazing," Ron says. "There was sort of someone watching over us," he adds.

No. It was pure luck—dumb, idiotic, inbred-toothless-country-boy-banjo-twangin' beginner's luck. I'll never do something like that again. I'm too old anyway.

With the Hitchhiker dead and Sally out of reach, Leatherface is steamed. And like any frustrated child, he wants to throw a tantrum. So, of course, it's time to dance.

Actually, Tobe had told me simply to stomp around as though really angry. The dance was just a bit of improvisation. (I attribute my success as a dancer to taking baton twirling in elementary school. It taught me to move gracefully while swinging awkward objects.)

Anyone not needed for the shot cleared out, since Daniel would be circling me as I vented. Tobe would be right next to Daniel, his head close to the camera. Wayne Bell would keep behind them as we moved, holding the boom overhead. Ted Nicolaou would be behind Wayne with his recorder. And we had to hurry. The sun was near the horizon, and we needed to shoot before it was gone.

Wayne was dancing before I was. "I was primed and ready for it," he says. "Not only am I trying to get the sound and not get hit, but also stay out of the camera and out of the cameraman's feet. So I'm his dancing partner whether he knows it or not." We must have looked odd, this big guy slamming around with a chain saw as four men circled him in lockstep.

I started stomping, slamming my feet down like a kid having a fit. I turned slowly as I stomped, and the foursome circled me. I don't think any of this looked very good at this point.

Daniel had no sense of the danger. "I'm into the camera, I'm in the finder, I'm in the moment of that movie, I'm oblivious to how close you're coming to me," he says. "I mean, when you're hand-holding with a wide-angle lens, you can bump into things you think are far away because they are much closer than they appear. So I'm basically just trying to hold the composition, that is, to hold you and the chain saw, I'm trying to keep the size of the shot, trying to get in the action. It wasn't until after we cut that everybody told me how close you'd come to hitting me with the saw. Of course your vision in that mask is limited, so I think the two of us . . . I don't think you were aware of how close you were coming to hitting me."

I had a rough idea.

At some point I raised the saw—like an angry kid might with something he's about to slam on the ground. When I turned, I glimpsed Tobe. He and his dancing partners were scuffling out of my way. Tobe knew I could barely see out of the mask. He knew he had to stay clear of me since in my blindness I might otherwise hit him. I spun around again to see what would happen. Peering through the mask's eye holes as I spun, I saw Tobe had moved away slightly.

New life entered me. *Tobe has to stay out of my way.* Now it was his turn to run from the chain saw. I decided to give him a real scare, to swing the saw at him. I was not angry at him for anything. But I was tired and, as we say these days, *so done* with this movie. For once I wanted to see Tobe scared. I wanted to be in control. I wanted to go home and be clean and rested.

The sun was setting. I started to dance.

I raised the saw and revved it into a snarl. I spun. I saw Tobe and took aim. This time he was going to have to stay out of my way.

I pirouetted as I swept the saw up.

Tobe and his crew shrank back from me.

I spun again and swung.

Tobe was mine.

CHAPTER 14

WE AIN'T IN NO HURRY, CUZ YOU AIN'T GOING NOWHERES

I do not really remember much after that. We wrapped for the day (well, forever, as far as I was concerned). I put on my real clothes and handed my stinking wardrobe to Dottie Pearl for the last time, after pocketing Leatherface's teeth as a token of my suffering. Then I drove home for that welcome shower and sleep. I don't think I saw any of the other *Chain Saw* gang for some weeks after that. I recall that I spent time catching up with friends, telling them as many crazy stories from the filming as I could muster up, trying to make sense of it all.

It took a long time for many of us to recover from shooting *Chain Saw*. The process itself had been so brutal that it used us up. We were physically exhausted and emotionally burned-out. Certainly no one on set was coddled. In fact, at times some of us felt that concern for our well-being extended only to keeping us filming; otherwise we were disposable. We were, as Bill Vail says, "so many sheep being sent to the slaughter." Even so, Bill is not complaining. "I was thrilled to make it," he says. "I just loved every second of it. I would do it again in a New York second."

"When I heard about what happened to the others, I got off

with a song, man," Allen Danziger says. His character, Jerry, was killed early on, so he was off the set before the worst of it. "It was fun for me. I had never been in a movie before—seeing all of that and just getting caught up in it. I felt, though, for the people that were doing the scene in that house."

Even after we'd wrapped, Marilyn Burns was again dealt the worst of it. Within two days of finishing, she got a call to come back and reshoot her escape in the truck. "That's when I lost it," she says. "I remember thinking I was done, so I came home that day and I got out of that nasty costume, that nasty shirt, and my hair was ruined, I was a mess. I was just kind of weepy for two days and going, 'Everybody just leave me alone.' Then right when I'm getting ready to say I'm okay, they call me and say, 'Marilyn, something went wrong with the footage. We're going to have to shoot the whole truck scene over.' And I had to come back in my little purple shirt; it's literally standing up. And then the pants are standing up. It's not easy to jump up in the truck. They made me do all the easy stuff."

But the worst for her? "Nobody said 'Good job.' Nobody ever complimented you," she says. "Nobody ever said a damn [bit of] praise. It was, 'Oh, okay, let's just go on to the next shot.' And that's how you felt every time. It worked real good on making you feel like hell, and I think that contributed to the film."

Some of us had wondered at times whether we would even finish the movie. Kim Henkel says he worried about that every day. "There were quite a few days," he says, "where I thought, *There's no way in hell we're going to get through this with anything that's worth doing anything [with], except sticking it in a shoe box and throwing it in the back of the closet.*"

Our minuscule budget made things worse. "It was early in my career and I wasn't smart enough to know to hire more people, just more PAs [Production Assistants], more bodies to help out," Ron Bozman says. "I was sort of functioning as assistant director. And also as production manager I was the one coordinating management for us. There was no one else. Kim was the one who produced it, keeping Tobe together and the actors in tow. But between him and me, we would deal with the whole thing. It was rough."

"I was up at five o'clock in the morning and then going till midnight," Kim says, "so it was grueling. I can't imagine it not being grueling for the cast as well, particularly toward the end; it was just devastating. Sometimes getting personnel on that set was difficult. Because of our budget, we didn't have any room to work with." Nowadays we call it guerrilla filmmaking, as if it were cool, but having a minimal crew is not sustainable over a long schedule. Everyone burns out.

"I can barely remember ten people or twelve people on the crew," Ted Nicolaou says. "Basically, we would just show up at the location, wait for Tobe and Kim to come and decide what they were going to shoot, and then figure out how to shoot it with our basic skills and equipment. The hardest parts were the endless heat and the kind of bare-minimal production support around us to make the film. But at the same time, we were so lucky and happy to be working on a film. It sort of just became this one long adventure for us. I can't remember more than Daniel and the gaffer and grip and me and an assistant and one makeup artist, and, God, it just seemed like the bare bones of a crew."

Kim says that the core of the crew always showed up ready for work. "The rest of it," he says, "was trying to herd cats. We had a lot of very inexperienced people, I think some very talented people, who had a lot to bring to the table, but a lot of times this was really the first dance for many of them, particularly doing a feature film. A lot of background experience but on a smaller scale, often student [films] or things like television spots or political spots or public service things, but very little feature experience. In fact, I don't know, other than if you consider *Eggshells* as a feature, I don't know anybody on that set who had any feature experience."

wrapping past dawn of the next day. The assistant cameraman, Lou Perryman—Lou, who could wax, not eloquent, but loquacious, loud, and larger than life about something—was pissing and moaning in a way that nobody else could do, performing outrage about this exasperating, difficult experience we'd just gone through [now that] we were all done and kind of letting out steam. Tobe happens to be walking by at just that moment and Lou was, 'how they had done it to us, how they had created this situation.' And he sees Tobe and he says, 'And there's the guy that did it, him right there!' And he goes up and he grabs Tobe, and he shakes him around, and he rolls on the ground with him. Tobe said later he assumed that Lou had broken, something had slipped in Lou, and that this could be it for Tobe Hooper. Lou is just, 'You, goddamn it, you, how could you do this to us? It's your fault, you little miserly so-and-so. Goddamn it!' Lou and Tobe had been good friends for quite a while. Now the steam has blown off, and Lou lets him up and, 'Oh, man, I'm sorry.' I understand now that was Lou's blessing, Lou's endorsement, Lou's certification that this was okay."

But, now that we had gone through this suffering, what did we really have to show for it? I had no idea. I was new to this and never even saw any footage during the filming, so I just hoped for the best.

Marilyn, on the other hand, was pretty positive. "We had a good scary movie," she says. "I loved horror movies and it was scary and we were good."

Still, many of us did not have her confidence.

" thought it was pretty crude and really had the look of dent film," Kim says. "And I was hoping we had enough to carry the day."

n't have a lot of confidence that it would be anything," an says. "It wouldn't have surprised me if it had just and nobody ever heard of it. It wouldn't have been a
"

There was a lot of editing to be done. Tobe and Larry edited in Tobe's living room. Larry would spend the day cutting together footage, and in the evenings Tobe would check it and recut parts. "Tobe was very inventive in the editing," Larry says, "and it took a lot of going back and forth and trying to figure out how to put it together."

Eventually they started seeing a movie emerging from their efforts. "We began to think, *Okay, this is something that's going to be something special*," Larry says. "But we never thought it was going to be earth-shattering, like everybody in the world was going to know about this film. We saw that it was really cool, and it would probably play at some drive-ins and maybe a few theaters that do horror films and the second-run theaters that existed back then."

During these early months, according to Wayne Bell, Sallye Richardson served as a kind of "general editing assistant" who "helped keep Larry in order." (She had been assistant director during the shooting.) When Larry had to leave the movie to go back to making a living—at two hundred dollars a week, he could not afford to keep working on the movie, he says—Sallye took over the editing, cutting it with Tobe. (There is a version of this story that has Sallye taking over and tossing out Larry's work because Tobe was not happy with Larry's editing. However, given Tobe's apparent reluctance to give credit, and Larry's shared credit with Sallye as editor on the final film, this version seems unlikely.)

Though he was not the sound editor, Wayne was responsible for much of the movie's sound design. He was in charge of post-production sound, including sound effects, and he also scored the film with Tobe. He calls their work "a *musique concrète* kind of score, and so it crosses over the line between what is sound effect and what is music." That eerie, whining camera-flash stinger heard when we glimpse the rotting corpses at the beginning is a sound effect; the deep, booming tone when Leatherface slams the metal door is part of the score. Wayne created both sounds.

Wayne had moved back into his parents' house for a few months during the editing to save money so he could stay available for the sound work. "I always had a recording studio with me, so my old bedroom became this funky recording area," he says. "I started to gather some of the sound-making devices I even have today, a lot that were used in *Chain Saw*. So it was in there that I recorded that stinger and a lot of other effects."

He adds, "A lot of the squeaking doors are doors from the house I grew up in, and the pig sounds that you hear, that's my father. There are cow sounds that you hear, and that's my father also."

When asked how he created the whining camera sound at the beginning of the movie, Wayne says, "Well, I'm holding on to that one. That's one of the most signature sounds in horror movies." He did explain to Tobe how he created the sound, but Tobe quickly forgot the details, which was fine with Wayne. "When I brought it to him, he just immediately responded, 'Oh, this is great!' I don't remember doing it specifically for that scene. In fact I almost got the impression that the sound gave him the inspiration for how to do the scene—the flash, the quick flashes. I don't know that for sure. But I invented this sound and brought it early on, and it was such an effective sound that it seems to me that he designed the scene around it."

Tobe and Wayne developed the score together, often in late-night jam sessions with a series of instruments, almost all of them Wayne's, including a lap steel guitar and a five-string double standing bass with a broken neck that he had glued back together. The other instruments included "lots of children's toy instruments, stuff made for preschoolers sometimes. A lot of the bone sounds, some of that is children's shaker toys," he says. As part of their music making, they did "a lot of bowing—we'd hang things on [the bass] for vibration, and so you hear that stand-up bass a lot, bowing of cymbals and bowing of other metallic things for the way they would ring."

"There were all kinds of just manipulation, playfulness with the score," he adds. "We had plenty of sessions of just play, before we actually started laying stuff down for the film. 'Let's do ice.' 'Let's do bones.' 'Let's do something about to happen, but not quite yet.' That kind of thing. And we would just pick up stuff. We had stuff scattered on the floor, and a lot of times we'd have slap-back tape echo. A variety of stuff, but all real world, no synthesizers."

The result of Wayne's work was a sound design that was new. Nothing like it had been heard before. "I think the sound in that movie makes it," director John Landis says.

As the editing continued, Tobe had to make some decisions about cutting scenes. Leatherface's makeup session, as I've mentioned, was cut from the "last supper." Tobe also streamlined the shredded-tent scene as Pam and Kirk approach the chain saw family house. He cut their finding the abandoned camp, leaving only a remnant shot showing the tent and the Dalí watch hanging with the other debris on the shrub while Kirk and Pam cross in the background without noticing it. He also cut my stomping in frustration once Sally escapes Leatherface at the gas station. Beyond the footage's looking lame, and its risk of diminishing the power of Leatherface's dance at the end by foreshadowing it, Tobe has said that he cut it because it was better for the audience not to know where Leatherface was at that moment.

Tobe also did the reverse, shooting additional footage as needed during editing. Aside from Marilyn's tortuous eyeball close-ups and her pickup truck escape, the crew filmed at a cattle feedlot in north Texas. This was for the cutaway shots of panting cattle when Pam, in the van, asks, "What's that smell?"

"It was in postproduction, too, when we shot the stills for the Hitchhiker at the slaughterhouse," Larry says. "Tobe and I and Sallye Richardson went out to take the photos. They would bring the first cow in to kill it and butcher it. It happened so fast I didn't get any pictures. You think it's going to take a while to do it, but those guys are *bang! bang! bang!* knocking them out. So it took some time to get the pictures. We walked out of there. Tobe and Sallye were both kind of reeling from the whole thing and saying, 'God, what do you want to do now?' 'Well, you guys are not going to believe this, but that barbecue next door just smells great.' I thought they were going to kill me. I didn't push the barbecue issue too much. I'd seen animals slaughtered before. It wasn't that I didn't have any idea where meat comes from."

The most significant addition in post was the new opening sequence set to Wayne's whining "stinger" sound effect, the camera flashes that slowly reveal decomposing, gooey body parts in the darkness, and then, in the dawn light, the grotesque sculpture—the rotting corpse impaled on the cemetery obelisk, a dripping head in its hands. At the same time we hear a radio report about grave robbing in the small town of Newt, Texas, which then expands to news of disasters and strange deaths throughout the country. The reason for adding this scene was simple. "The opening stank," Marilyn says. "The kids in the van, we looked like idiots."

"The film just didn't have a good opening," Larry says, more diplomatically. "Of course we had to do something that didn't cost anything." Warren Skaaren, the head of the Texas Film Commission and long-term friend of this movie, came up with the new shots.

"That was really kind of fun, shooting that graveyard scene," Kim says. "I built that gravestone out of two-by-fours and drywall, and painted it to look like a granite stone or marble monument. Then the actual creature on top of it, the cadaver: Warren Skaaren actually constructed that guy. He'd been a sculpture student at Rice. He did the basics on the character that's on there, and then we did the finish on it."

Warren used a human skeleton as an armature, building it up into a body using mostly wax and clay. This would have been the same skeleton that Bob Burns had bought as set dressing. Part of Kim's finishing work, apparently, was then to pour transmission fluid over it for that drippy sheen.

Then, Kim says, "We all went out to Leander Cemetery at the crack of dawn one day and shot that." As for getting permission to shoot, "Well, stealing locations is a sport in independent filmmaking."

"We went out there with a boom arm that Ron Perryman [assistant cameraman Lou Perryman's brother] had devised to do the shot," Wayne says. "It plays as sunrise, but was shot at sunset. I remember Ron being very clear that this is going to be a great sunset. Ron was an excellent still photographer and had a lot of experience in photography. You could tell this one was going to be great, and indeed it was this wonderfully blood-red sunset to reveal that bizarre sculpture."

Sunrise or sunset, we no longer worry about such minor contradictions in our *Chain Saw* story.

Once the new opening was shot, Tobe's editing of this sequence was all about timing and visual perception. "I wanted the beginning of *Chain Saw* to really grab you by the throat," he says in his interview with Paolo Zelati. "So you get these flashes of light that would last—probably they were four frames, so that would be about a quarter of a second, and then to darkness. Those images would just retain in the retina of your eye. Then gradually you started seeing teeth, then you put together, 'Okay, this is a dead body.' Then there's a hand that flashes. I'd repeat the flash three times, and there's a hand pointing toward another hand, and I believe there's a ring on the corpse's finger, I think. So there's so much you can do with one frame. Because in the horror genre something that makes you jump, it comes down to that fiftieth of a second, and that fiftieth of a second has to be just at the right place at the right time. But anyway it was all about the bright and the dark."

Stuart Gordon is particularly impressed with this opening. "You're seeing these shots of body parts, and it looks like it's the real deal," he says. "It really does. I don't know where that footage came from or what that was, exactly. But it sets up the audience for this—you're going to see something that's real."

"Tobe had great strength as an editor," Wayne says. "A very good editor, very understanding of when that moment is to cut away or cut into something, and how to string cuts together to create more energy than was actually there."

This tight editing that takes fractions of a second into consideration corresponds closely with Tobe's thinking when he cut together the last scene, Sally's escape and Leatherface's dance. "When I shot it I didn't know if I would end it on her screaming," he says. "I didn't know if I would end it on the chain saw dance, but I was cutting it, and I found this perfect moment where he, Leatherface, swings the saw back and almost hits the camera, and I cut to black. It's in the middle of action that's already rolling, so it just stops, then there's nothing. It seems like it's about eighteen frames, maybe one second, of black before the credits roll. There's enough black there, it stops so the sound compression is still in your head, so you can feel you've gone to nothing." I am glad I decided to take that swing at Tobe.

And as these elements came together and the movie took shape as a whole, they began to feel that they had something here. And that something was very new.

"I know there was a certain point in the editing process when we really began to realize that this was not the movie that we thought we were going to make," Larry says. "This was a different animal. There wasn't anything like it. The closest thing was *Night of the Living Dead* [1968], but it was not like what the other horror films were at the time; they'd done nothing like it. We knew this was really, really, different. That was one of the reasons I think people hated *Texas Chain Saw Massacre*, because they felt like we had really done something."

We were lucky. Tobe and the gang had turned this mess into a real movie.

CHAPTER 15

AMERICA'S MOST BIZARRE AND BRUTAL CRIMES

After waiting more than a year for *Leatherface*'s release we found out that it had become *The Texas Chain Saw Massacre*—and was being promoted as a true story.

I was dismayed and disappointed. How could they put such a sleazy title on my—okay, *our*—little horror movie? And what was this opening scroll about the terrible things that happened to Sally Hardesty on August 18, 1973? We were *filming* on that night. Besides, the story had been made up. (John Larroquette, an unknown actor at the time, narrated those lines about "the most bizarre crimes in the annals of American history.")

Kim Henkel says that *Leatherface* had never been the intended title. It was nothing more than a placeholder, something to use while we were shooting, just as *Headcheese* was its working title for a while during the writing. Looking back, I suppose that *Headcheese* was never really going to be the title, either. All this time, Tobe, Kim, and the other producers had been looking for something better.

Warren Skaaren had come up with the new name, reportedly during a late-night poker game. "He called me up one morning,"

Ron Bozman says. "I was in Houston and he said, 'I've got it!' I said, 'What?' '*Texas Chain Saw Massacre*.' 'You do, you do have it. That's it! That's brilliant!'"

"It's one of those kinds of things that once you say it, it's obvious," Kim Henkel says. "What else would you call it?"

"I thought *Oh my God, this is great*," Mary Church says.

I, for one, would have called it *Leatherface*. But of course I had a personal interest in that name. Wayne Bell hated the idea that Texas would be "branded like this," but he quickly came around.

Okay, I admit I was very wrong. Of course, I understood nothing about marketing. Changing the title was the single smartest move they made to promote the movie.

"I think the title was a huge part of its popularity," Ron says. "At least in getting people into the theater. Then the movie itself took over. But it was such a brilliant, out-of-the-box idea."

The *Chain Saw* name sold the movie before anyone walked into a theater.

And creating the notion of its being a real story also seemed to make the movie more compelling—as if the audience needed this little lie to suspend their disbelief and make the experience more "real." We would eventually see this it-really-happened pitch repeated with other fictional scares, from *The Last House on the Left* (1972) to *The Amityville Horror* (1979) to *The Blair Witch Project* (1999) to *Paranormal Activity* (2007), until it became a cliché of small-budget movie marketing worthy of the great horror producer and promoter William Castle. (For us, though, this deception had unintended consequences—an entire mythos has grown up about the "real" killings the movie is based on.)

Finally, on October 11, 1974, *The Texas Chain Saw Massacre* was released in two hundred theaters throughout the South and parts of the Southwest, including, of course, Texas. (The movie was released regionally, its two hundred prints traveling around the country over many months.) I do not know whether our movie had an official premiere. Teri believes that Marilyn, Ed, Tobe, and

Kim went to a private screening at a theater in downtown Austin, to which she was not invited. But no one seems to remember this screening. I certainly was not there.

A number of people did see the movie in Austin. Allen Danziger says that when he saw the trailer for it some days beforehand, he "went into a panic attack and went running out of the theater." But he did see it on opening night, riding to a theater in north Austin with friends who had rented a limo for the occasion. "It grabbed me," he says. "You're looking at yourself: *How do I look? How am I coming? Are you phony in it? Is it believable?* And I didn't know how everybody died. As I say, I wasn't on set other than my stuff." Otherwise, he says, he was not impressed with the movie.

John Dugan was back to his theater life in Chicago when he saw it for the first time. "I thought it was terrific," he says. "We had a lot of walkers out of that theater. When Teri McMinn gets hung on the meat hook, I'd say 25 percent of the theater got up and walked out. Just like, *Okay, that's enough of that.*"

Marilyn, in Los Angeles pursuing her acting career, saw it in a Hollywood screening room where the producers were trying to sell it to a distributor. From the beginning she had feared that somehow she would be left on the cutting room floor, even though she was the main character. It had already happened to her with small roles in *Lovin' Molly* and *Brewster McCloud*, and surely it would happen again. "That's what I worried about when I actually viewed the picture for the first time. *I'm still in it, I'm still in it, oh good, thank God,*" she says. "I wanted it so much, and I believed in it." Marilyn thought the movie was pretty good. The distributor, however, turned it down.

John Landis first saw it at a Hollywood Boulevard grind house. "I knew nothing about it other than it had a kind of tacky poster and an insane exploitation title," he says. "I thought, *Oh my God!* First of all, it was terrifying, and also it was funny. That was the thing, I don't know if people talk about that or not, but it was funny. There was shit in it that was really funny. Also really tragic, and completely successfully a nightmare in that this girl is . . . you're trapped with her throughout. It's relentless, the movie's relentless. That movie really, really had a profound impact on me."

Bill Vail was let down, at least at first. He had moved to New York and had a chance to see it before the release. "Tobe came up there with the final cut to do color corrections and make the final print," Bill says. "So he said, 'C'mon, let's go to dinner, and then we will come over and see the movie.' We saw it, and my immediate reaction was I was so disappointed. I don't know what I was expecting, but what I got wasn't it. It was totally disappointing to me." He realized later that he was focusing on his own performance, not the movie overall. When he saw it again, this time in a theater off Times Square, "it was more impressive," he says. Maybe the screams from the audience helped.

I saw it at a theater in south Austin. A bunch of us went—all friends out for a fun evening. We gathered in the parking lot before the show, and the gang presented me with an ancient chain saw and the charter of the Gunnar Hansen Fan Club announcing the "World Premiere of *The Texas Chainsaw Massacre*." It was our sort of premiere. The charter was signed by everyone there—in red ink, of course.

I convinced the theater manager that I had actually been in the movie, so he let me in free. We trooped in and filled two or three rows in a back corner, joking among ourselves before the movie started. I remember that people were looking at us, wondering, I guess, why we were so noisy and excited. Several rows directly in front of us, four girls in their late teens looked back at us and giggled.

All our work had come together for this moment. The movie unrolled before the audience, chronicling Leatherface and his grisly family with a fondness for sausage and certain tools. I loved it. It was so much more than what I had expected during those long, exhausting days on set. My heart was racing, not because I was scared—I already knew the entire story a bit too well for that—but because I was so caught up in *Chain Saw*'s pacing. This was not one of those talky, tiresome teenager horror movies we suffered through in those days. This movie delivered. I remember the screams in the theater. People walked out. But the audience that stayed was hooked.

As the movie ground on, I noticed that the four teenagers were sliding lower and lower in their seats. Now and then one of them would slowly turn and look back at us, but this time in fear. Finally they had slid so low that when one of them turned I could see only her eyes and the top of her head. When the lights came on the four jumped up and scuttled past us and out into the safety of the night. They did not look at us.

———•———

This movie would be big, and I was in it. My life would be very different now, and all my suffering would be worth it. I would be Somebody. Well, that overstates it, but I had hopes.

Many people now call *Chain Saw* a cult movie, but it never really was. It was too successful. It was getting big attention and making money almost immediately. People were going to the movie in large numbers, and they certainly were talking about it.

"The movie was pretty much instantaneously huge," Daniel Pearl says. "I remember being in restaurants and hearing people talking about it at other tables near me, talking about the film. I remember turning up my television, and on the news they were talking about the film."

One of its first reviews was in the University of Texas student newspaper, *The Daily Texan*. The writer sort of liked the movie, saying "*The Texas Chain Saw Massacre* is a good little horror movie." Faint praise, maybe, but still praise.

The *Hollywood Reporter* also liked it: "Made in Austin, Texas, largely by some very talented graduate students of the University of Texas, this Vortex/Henkel/Hooper Production is thoroughly professional, compelling, and gruesome," the reviewer wrote. "Squarely within the traditions of the *Psycho* genre, it is a fresh and extreme interpretation that should do for meat-eating what Hitchcock did for shower-taking." That was better.

Most critics were not so kind, however.

Johnny Carson, on the *Tonight Show*, hated it. I watched him one night as he ranted about the movie, getting angrier as he went. Though I do not remember his exact words, essentially he said that *Chain Saw* was junk and should have received an X rating, not an R.

Linda Gross in the *Los Angeles Times* called it a "despicable film. . . . Craziness handled without sensitivity is a degrading, senseless, misuse of film and time." There were plenty more, just as brutal.

Ed Neal saw what may be the most high-toned bad review, from a critic in London. "He wrote, 'Well, as for the Hitchhiker, the only thing I can tell you is that he's a perfectly insidious lout,'" Ed says. "I'd never been called a lout before. I had to look it up."

Maybe these critics just hated *Chain Saw* because it was so unpleasant.

But New York critic Rex Reed liked it, calling it the most horrifying picture he had ever seen, more frightening than *Night of the Living Dead*. One newspaper ad for the movie, exploiting his comments, had added the tag: "Unparalleled terror —Rex Reed."

Roger Ebert in Chicago also liked it, though with reservations: ". . . a real Grand Guignol of a movie. It's also without any apparent purpose, unless the creation of disgust and fright is a purpose. And yet in its own way, the movie is some kind of weird, off-the-wall achievement. I can't imagine why anyone would want to make a movie like this, and yet it's well-made, well-acted, and all too effective." He also said, "*The Texas Chainsaw Massacre* belongs in a select company (with *Night of the Living Dead* and *Last House on the Left*) of films that are really a lot better than the genre requires." Though he added: "Not, however, that you'd necessarily enjoy seeing it."

Of course all this attention, good or bad, only drew more viewers to the theaters.

It was making money. Bryanston Distributing, the distributor, ran a full page ad in the October 16th issue of industry trade magazine *Variety*, claiming that *Chain Saw* had grossed $602,133 in Texas alone in its first four days ("outgrossing the record-breaking *Return of the Dragon!*"). It was doing "socko" business in Chicago, premiering with $40,000 at the end of October, and by November 5th the trade estimated a "lightning $67,500 premiere" on ten screens in L.A. The film cracked *Variety*'s list of the fifty top-grossing films for the week ending October 23 at number thirty-nine, right above the Blacksploitation movie *Foxy Brown* and right below the Ingmar Bergman film *Scenes from a Marriage*. All the numbers we were hearing were big.

That convinced me. This movie would, indeed, be big. And I was going to be a Movie Star and I was going to be rich.

————•————

Instead, things just got weird.

The first odd thing about being part of the movie world was getting a call from my old boss, the one who had fired me from my bartending job the year before and freed me to work on the movie. He wanted to get together for lunch at one of his restaurants.

He was very friendly when we met, but just talked about nothing much. Finally he got to the point. He was opening a new bar in Austin and he wanted an investor, a silent partner. That investor could be me.

He thought that I must be rich now, being a Movie Star and all. I was not. *Yet*. But I knew then that when I did become rich from this movie, my money would not go to him.

Then a friend decided that I should put my stardom to good use. I should meet some fans. Well, one fan in particular. She was, it seems, impressed by fame. One night we drove to her apartment. She was lovely, though she was not particularly impressed with me until my friend pointed out that I had been in *that movie*.

She suggested we go see it together. I happily agreed.

We went the next night. When I picked her up, she was in a state of excitement that almost matched mine. I think she was slightly breathless. She suggested a quick drink before the movie, with a promise of some fun in front of the fireplace afterward.

I liked where this was going.

She rubbed against me when we drove off to experience *The Texas Chain Saw Massacre*. Close together in the darkness we watched me on the screen. We watched as I clubbed Kirk with my hammer. We watched as I hung Pam on the hook, and as I carved pitiful Franklin in two. We watched as my roaring saw and I chased Sally through the woods and into the clutches of the Cook. We watched as my family and I tortured Sally during the endless dinner. And we watched me dance in frustration when Sally escaped.

She was strangely quiet on the way home. Not that I noticed at the time. I was busy thinking about my upcoming adventures by her fireplace.

She fished her key out of her pocket as we approached her door, and then she slid it into the lock. She turned toward me and said something like, "It was interesting." Before I could give her my Movie Star smile, she stepped through the door and slammed it shut. Quite firmly.

I realized then that stardom was not going to be quite what I expected. Surely Peter Fonda had had an easier time of it after *Easy Rider* came out.

But I could live with that. Money would ease a lot of pain.

In the meantime, the months went by. I basked in the glory of *Chain Saw*'s growing notoriety and speculated at times with Allen and Ed about our pending movie wealth. In the meantime I continued teaching, though I do not think that any of my freshmen students associated their teaching assistant with *that* Gunnar Hansen.

We waited for our share of the money. When we wondered why it had not arrived, Kim told us that everything in the movie business worked in ninety-day cycles and that it would take at least three months.

Those three months came and went. Nothing. Six months. Nothing.

We kept hearing how well the movie was doing. Bryanston was advertising big sales—in the millions.

In May of 1975, *Chain Saw* was screened at the Cannes Film Festival, as part of the Director's Fortnight (*Quinzaine des Réalisateurs*), a showcase of new directors and independent and avant-garde films presented out of competition and in parallel to the main festival. When I ask Kim Henkel how *Chain Saw* got there, he says simply, "That's a mystery to me; I have no clue, no clue."

Other films in that year's series included Rainer Werner Fassbinder's *Faustrecht der Freiheit* and Chantal Akerman's *Jeanne Dielman, 23 Quai du Commerce*; the other American film shown was *Milestones*, an ambitious epic of post-counterculture America by Robert Kramer and John Douglas. (The year before, one of the two American films shown was Martin Scorsese's *Mean Streets*.) According to the film's short program note at the time:

"*The Texas Chainsaw Massacre* is based on a true story that took place in Wisconsin twenty years ago. This is a film about 'meat,' about people who go beyond eating the flesh of animals, of rats, of dogs, of cats. These are mentally retarded people, crazy people, people who we do not know ultimately if they are human or animal."

In *Lost in the Garden of the World*, a documentary made at the Cannes Festival that year, the filmmaker, talking to director Paul Bartel (*Death Race 2000*), says that everyone who saw *Chain Saw* at Cannes, ". . . adored it, adored it!" Bartel nods, and says, "And *Chain Saw Massacre* goes in for unrelieved terror and suspense."

In the same documentary, Tobe speaks a bit about why he made *Chain Saw*. With assistant cameraman Lou Perryman standing behind him grinning, Tobe says, "I lost a lot of my best friends just beginning the project. They said, 'Wait around, wait around for the next project.' And some of those people have been waiting for fifteen years. And so I wanted to get about my career. The next film will be much tamer. I feel my range is broad enough to get into depth in most anything I want to do. In the States, for a very well-made artistic film, you have about six hundred theaters across the country, whereas *Chain Saw* has thousands. And what this means to me is another job."

Six months later, it was screened at the London Film Festival, and won the "Critic's Choice" award.

Then we heard through our informal grapevine that the Museum of Modern Art in New York had placed a copy in its permanent collection and had screened it as part of their Re/View program.

(Described by MoMA as providing another opportunity for viewers to see "pictures that surfaced briefly only to disappear before finding an audience" the program also included other recent American films such as Elia Kazan's *The Visitors*, Robert Altman's *Thieves Like Us*, Jonathan Demme's *Caged Heat*, Ossie Davis's *Black Girl*, and Peter Yates's *The Friends of Eddie Coyle*. MoMA hadn't actually purchased the film: according to Bob Burns, apparently someone from Bryanston had donated a print.)

Not coincidentally, Bryanston was very quickly afterwards touting our MoMA connection. Not only was the movie popular, it was also being recognized—by these people, at least—as Art. Surely, we kept thinking, our money must be piling up somewhere.

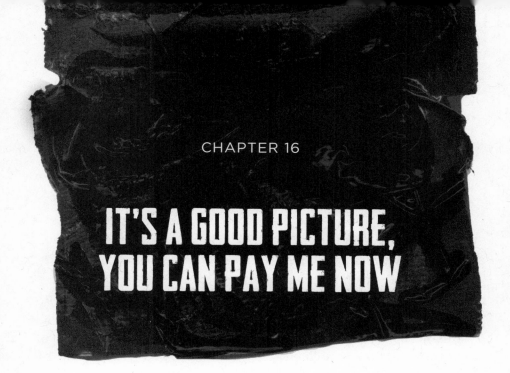

CHAPTER 16

IT'S A GOOD PICTURE, YOU CAN PAY ME NOW

"You have one shot at the brass ring," Allen Danziger says. "And so, here, when that movie came out, I'm watching *Variety*, I'm seeing this has got a bullet, this movie's grossing this. I said this is my retirement account, you know, four million, six million, whatever."

Some of the gang started spending that yet-to-be-paid money. One actor told me that he and his wife had bought a houseful of furniture in anticipation of a large payment.

Maybe I should have started worrying when one of the crew said to me, "I don't know why they went with a Mafia distributor."

Finally, on July 3, 1975, nine months after the movie's release, we got our first checks.

Mine was for $47.07. (This after a $800 salary, about $2 an hour, for four long weeks of shooting.)

Something was wrong.

Just looking at the statement with this payment, I could see things were not as I had thought. I owned a small share in Vortex, which I believed owned the movie. But of the money that came in, before any went to Vortex, half had gone to some company named

M.A.B., controlled by Jay Parsley. (Parsley once joked that M.A.B. stood for "Marilyn A. Burns," but Marilyn says that he had no reason to name it after her, and it must have stood for something else entirely.) Then 19 percent of what was left went to some company called P.I.T.S. (which we learned stood for Pie in the Sky). That meant that Vortex owned only about 40 percent of the movie, not the whole thing. And by the time assorted indecipherable fees were siphoned off from this $24,282.74 payment, Vortex's share to distribute was a mere $8,100—about 33 percent of the money. So my already small share was worth a third of what I had expected.

On top of that, why had the payment from Bryanston been so small to begin with? Why, if the movie was making millions, as they claimed, was their payment only twenty-four thousand dollars instead of a couple million?

You get the picture. We were not going to get rich.

It was a disaster for some of the gang. For me it did not matter so much—I had a job and no debts. But I certainly could have used that money.

———————

The story of *Chain Saw*'s money has been told before, though these accounts vary so much that it is hard to know which details are true. So I will just summarize briefly what I know. Understanding the money story does not give us insight into what *Chain Saw* is about or why it has been so successful. Still, it is part of the movie's mythology, and it serves as some kind of cautionary tale.

This is really two stories: the way the film was financed, and the way our money was handled by the distributor. Neither story is heartwarming.

Ron Bozman, who had roomed with Kim on *Windsplitter*, had introduced Tobe and Kim to his old college roommate Warren Skaaren, the director of the Texas Film Commission, one of a number of people they approached to help sort out *Chain Saw*'s initial financing. Skaaren, in turn, connected them with Jay Parsley, who had invested in other movies. Parsley said he would raise the sixty thousand dollars they needed and produce the movie in exchange for half ownership. The rest belonged to Vortex, that is, Tobe and Kim. Parsley put up forty thousand dollars himself, becoming *Chain Saw*'s principal investor. The remaining twenty thousand dollars came from several sources, including lawyer Bob Kuhn and a bag of cash from Daniel Pearl's drug-dealer friend.

Ron says that there was an additional thirty-five thousand or so in deferments—commitments made for services that would be paid for when the movie started making money. But that was not cash. So when the production started running low on money during the editing, Vortex raised more.

This time they worked with Austin attorney Joe Longley, then chief of the antitrust and consumer-protection division of the Texas attorney general's office. He put together a meeting with a group of cash-heavy friends who played poker together. By the end of the meeting, people were writing checks, including $2,000 from Longley, himself. They called their group Pie in the Sky, a not reassuring name. But then they did not need to make money. "We thought this movie was going to be such a dog that we'd all get a good tax write-off," Longley told the *Los Angeles Times* nine years later. For P.I.T.S.'s $23,532, Tobe and Kim signed over 19 percent of Vortex.

The result was that we minor shareholders held a fraction of what we thought we had. And no one who signed away those percentages ever bothered to tell us.

About the time that *Chain Saw* was looking for a distributor, Warren left the Film Commission and became the producers' rep—he would sell the movie. For this he negotiated with the producers a five-thousand dollar deferred salary and 15 percent of Vortex. And he would receive a "monitoring fee" of 3 percent of the combined Vortex and M.A.B. profits. None of us knew about this, either.

Warren had approached almost every studio in Hollywood to seek distribution for *Chain Saw*, with no luck.

"I think one of the reasons it didn't fly was they didn't want to take a gamble on an independent 16mm film from Texas," Marilyn says. "As good a film as it was, it wasn't in the industry. It was made outside Hollywood. Everybody wanted to see it, everybody was curious about it. The word of mouth was going around, but everybody was afraid of touching it."

That left Bryanston, a new company in Hollywood founded by two brothers, Joseph and Louis "Butchie" Peraino. They had made millions from financing and distributing *Deep Throat* (1972), and had gone on to produce and distribute the notorious *Andy Warhol's Frankenstein* (1973) and distribute Bruce Lee's penultimate film *Return of the Dragon* (1972), further capitalizing on the release after his death when the major studios had turned it down. They were also rumored to be part of the Joseph Colombo crime family in New York.

Their initial offer was quite a bit more than the cost of making *Chain Saw,* so the investors and deferred debts could be paid off right away. Warren and Ron and their lawyers went to Bryanston's New York office to negotiate the details directly with Louis and Joseph.

"There was this big old Cadillac outside and some big, burly guys in suits leaning against it—I mean like the guards," Ron says. "We went upstairs, and around a table were these other big, burly guys in suits. It's really like something out of those mob movies. We're sitting there and a guy comes in . . . with some jewelry on a little tray . . . and then one of the brothers says, 'It's for the wife.' It's her birthday or their anniversary or something. 'Yeah, we'll take that.' And then they bring in this Italian spread of antipasto. And so it was just this scene out of the *Godfather* around the table. It was just rich beyond words."

They left with a contract for $225,000 and 35 percent of the distribution profits.

No more money came in for a long time, in spite of the big money talk in the trades. In less than a year, *Variety* was reporting that *Chain Saw* had grossed more than twelve million dollars. Yet, according to a September 1982 *Los Angeles Times* article, in the four quarterly financial statements that Bryanston sent in the first year and a half, they claimed a gross income from the film of only $1,082,422. However, according to a former Bryanston employee, the company had made six million dollars on it in its first fourteen months. Our share of that should have been more than two million dollars.

In the middle of all this, the minor shareholders were meeting with the producers to find out why there was so little money. But no one was telling us much about what was going on. Ed Neal was particularly angry when we found out about Warren's fees and his new share of Vortex. There were heated meetings and hard feelings.

I asked one of the other shareholders how we could have agreed to such a bad contract with the distributor. She looked at me like I was the innocent that I was. "It doesn't matter how good the contract is," she said. "If they don't want to pay you, they're not going to pay you."

Eventually we would all come to call the Perainos "the Piranhas."

In May 1976, a year and a half after the film's release, the producers filed a federal suit for breach of contract against Bryanston. Of course, the movie continued to make money as the suit dragged on. Finally, getting nowhere, nine months later the producers decided to cut their losses and accept Bryanston's offer of four hundred thousand dollars and control of the film. Though this was a fraction of the millions that Bryanston owed us, at least it meant that, with the film back, the producers could find new distribution and start over. The federal judge approved the settlement.

But we never got even that money. Bryanston by this point had none. And the film's prints and distribution rights were in the hands of creditors and distributors who were not about to relinquish anything without payment from the producers.

Then the lawsuits really started piling up, mostly between the producers and the different companies to which Bryanston had surreptitiously licensed some part of *Chain Saw*'s rights. Kim and Tobe even sued Jay Parsley and Bob Kuhn, the lawyer who had represented the movie in the original federal suit, this time for trying to negotiate a new distribution deal for *Chain Saw* without involving the filmmakers. In addition, Kuhn was claiming 25 percent of all past and future profits of the film. Reportedly, in the eight years after *Chain Saw*'s release, more than twenty-five suits were filed.

The only one of the cast or crew to sue anyone was Bob Burns, who filed against the producers, in spite of his long friendship with Tobe. He ended up getting a modest settlement. "I think there were a couple of issues," Mary Church says of Bob's suit. "I think, financially, he felt everything had been mishandled, which it had been, and so by rights that film could have set all of them up for life, maybe a frugal life, but a life. [The film's] cost versus its cash intake was substantial. Bob was not very happy with the aftermath."

Eventually a federal judge in Austin ordered that all *Chain Saw* money be held by the court until the squabbling stopped. Finally, in 1981, the producers got *Chain Saw* back. In those seven years, beyond paying back the investors, the movie reportedly made only about forty-five thousand dollars in profit. This from a supposed twenty million dollar gross its first two years.

Chain Saw grossed another six million in its 1981 re-release, and since then has continued to generate money through box office and video sales, sequel rights, and merchandising of various *Chain Saw* tchotchkes (including *Chain Saw* lunchboxes, t-shirts, clocks, facsimile posters, aprons, masks, and toy chain saws, as well as countless different Leatherface action figures). The home video release entered the *Billboard* top 40 sales chart at number twenty-three (just under Richard Pryor's *Bustin' Loose*) the day before Valentine's Day, 1982, and spent twenty-five weeks on the chart before falling off in early August. But in the four decades since *Chain Saw*'s release, my share in Vortex has produced only about eight thousand dollars.

The worst part for me was not that I made little money from the movie—I had not expected to make any at all. The worst was that, whatever amount the movie made, there should have been enough for everyone.

Nobody is particularly happy with the way things worked out. "I don't think [the producers] knew, and I don't think they did it out of malice," Allen says. "But that movie supposedly took in so much money that you'd have thought that more could have been done for the actors to kind of make it right. They had, to me, so many opportunities to make it right. It looks like everybody was shafted."

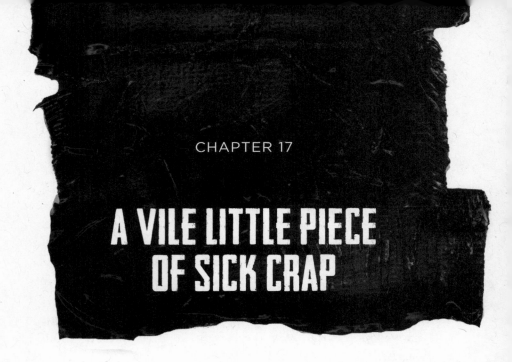

CHAPTER 17

A VILE LITTLE PIECE OF SICK CRAP

It was quickly obvious that, despite *Chain Saw*'s popularity, many people, including most critics, hated it. And that hatred ran deep. As the movie got more attention and became better known, the hatred just increased. The fact that it had been well received in some high cultural circles seemed to elevate it from an object of disdain to some kind of threat.

David Robinson's review in *The Times* of London in November 1976 is emblematic of the feeling at the time: "The less said about Tobe Hooper's *The Texas Chain Saw Massacre* the better, perhaps, though I must take my share of the blame for calling attention to the film after its first European screenings at the Cannes Festival in 1975. . . . The fact that it is rather efficiently and effectively done only makes the film more unpalatable."

In a June 1981 *New York Times* article entitled "When Movies Take Pride in Being Second-Rate," Vincent Canby took particular exception with *Chain Saw*'s being in MoMA. "*The Texas Chainsaw Massacre* is being advertised as having been 'selected' for the Museum of Modern Art's permanent collection. A MoMA spokesman says the permanent collection is for films the museum decides are timeless works of art. A print of *The Texas Chainsaw Massacre* has been given to the museum to be part of its 'study collection,' which is something else entirely," he sniffed. (Canby soon after seemed to soften his stance, writing three months later about the film, "The intelligence at work within it transforms the second-rate into an unexpectedly provocative entertainment.")

But the most brutal and most famously venomous criticism of *Chain Saw* came from Stephen Koch in his article "Fashions in Pornography," published in *Harper's Magazine* in November 1976. He did not merely hate the movie. He despised it.

> *The Texas Chain Saw Massacre* is a vile little piece of sick crap which opened early in 1974 in a nameless Times Square exploitation house, there to be noticed only as another symptom of the wet rot, another step along the way. . . . It is a particularly foul item in the currently developing hard-core pornography of murder . . . designed to milk a few more bucks out of the throng of shuffling wretches who still gather, every other seat, in those dank caverns for the scab-picking of the human spirit which have become so visible in the worst sections of the central cities.

So: he did not like it. But immediately after this overheated passage, Koch identified his real enemy: not the film ("trash"), nor the shuffling wretches who see it, but film buffs:

> Yet placed before its intended audience, *The Texas Chain Saw Massacre* was a complete failure. Unfortunately, it did not then proceed to die the death it deserved. At the last minute it was suddenly and, it would seem, inexplicably rescued by a certain branch of the film intelligentsia, who sent it sailing down the high road to fame and influence. And it has gone on to great things. The first phase was a sudden fashion among the film buffs, some of whom latched on to the picture with the enthusiasm that suggests that film buffery, that beguiling beacon of Sixties taste, has slid into some really desperate final phase.

The majority of the piece then goes on to attack this scourge of film buffery ("buff taste seems to have been steadily moving towards bankruptcy"), which saved this sick piece of crap from financial disaster (pure fantasy on Koch's part) and allowed the barbarians to scale the walls of MoMA and Cannes. Koch's hatred for the film—and boy, does he hate it—does not let up.

"It is a film with literally nothing to recommend it: nothing but a hysterically paced, slapdash, imbecile concoction of cannibalism, voodoo, astrology, sundry hippie-esque cults, and unrelenting sadistic violence as extreme and hideous as a complete lack of imagination can possibly make it." He called the movie "simultaneously unpleasant and unimportant." Not only that, it was banal and barely competent technically. In fact it was comically inept. He clumped us together as "despicable little makers of this despicable little movie." He imagined that he had seen multiple Leatherfaces ("obese gibbering castrati"; I actually like that one) and then the fantasies really took over, as he started ranting about "self-immolations" and "hysterical necrophilia."

Of course, in the middle of all this, he got in his shots at the movie's tenuous MoMA and Cannes connections. It was important for him to establish that they were certainly not legitimate. For some reason MoMA and Cannes seemed to really gall critics.

Koch's title dismisses all of the popular interest in the movie as some kind of fashion, that is, as something superficial and short-lived. I guess he is trusting on a little misdirection here, that we are too busy huffing and puffing about the "pornography" part to spot the fashion insult. And as for the pornography charge, an issue often raised about horror movies, Koch teeters on calling *Chain Saw* a snuff movie. Yet it seems an unlikely candidate for such charges. He also calls liking the movie a kind of "bufferism," likely an extreme form of being a film buff, which he dismisses as a withered branch of intellectualism.

(I cannot resist mentioning here that Koch is the author of the 1973 book *Stargazer: Andy Warhol's World and His Films*, which he dedicates "to the pale master." Also released in 1973 was *Andy Warhol's Frankenstein*, which was given an X by the MPAA for sex and violence, and actually does include necrophilia, as well as a disembowelment scene made all the more graphic for those lucky enough to see the film in its 3D release. Coincidentally, the film was also distributed by Bryanston.)

Koch's piece drew a response by critic Roger Greenspun in the January-February 1977 issue of *Film Quarterly*, notable for how each writer uses his response to *Chain Saw* for his own purpose. Greenspun is no particular fan of the movie. In fact he seems deliberately to be playing it sort of cool to Koch's amped-up vitriol. ("There's no point in pretending that *The Texas Chain Saw Massacre* hides a secret life in which it is something other than, or 'better' than, it means to be. . . . The problem—I mean this—is that there seems to be nothing of interest here.") He also corrects a number of errors in Koch's piece, but calls this "beside the point." He's really here to challenge Koch's "damnable conspiracy involving low-budget filmmakers, MoMA, and the whole dismal history of film-buff taste." So *Chain Saw* is either threatening trash, or there's nothing about it "of interest." Had they seen the same movie?

Indeed, Koch's criticisms are so broad-stroked and his specifics so inaccurate that one wonders whether he ever saw the movie at all. That's often the case with those who hate *Chain Saw*.

This anger about *Chain Saw* extends beyond the film critics who dislike its subject or its technique. It is also taken up by those who want to blame the movie for all of society's ills. In their view, it is both the cause of violence and a corruptor of children.

My first encounter with this phenomenon came at a chamber music concert one summer evening in 1975. An older woman whom I knew vaguely came up to me. She said something like, "Sixteen people were murdered today in New York City, and it is *your* fault." Hyperbole aside, she was not joking.

I was flummoxed by her statement. What in the world was she talking about? It was *that movie*. Apparently seeing *The Texas Chain Saw Massacre*, according to her, was inspiring empty-souled viewers to kill and to kill in volume, increasing New York's murder rate. As Leatherface, I was somehow responsible.

Over the years, all of us from *Chain Saw* have repeatedly faced some variant of this statement. And people's need to make a point about this has not eased over time. The most extreme incident for me came in 2002 in North Carolina, where I was making a Halloween season appearance. I was asked to come to the University of North Carolina at Pembroke to talk to a class. I agreed, though it seemed odd that I was being asked to talk horror movies to a pre-law class.

This college was in the digital age, it turned out, and the class was being streamed over the Internet to classrooms throughout the state system. The professor was very friendly. He also had an agenda.

His first, and only, question was, "How can you justify the violence in *Chain Saw* in the face of growing violence in American society?" Oh, my God! A trap! Caught in front of an audience of thousands—okay, tens—and forced to stumble through an answer! That professor was one clever devil.

He was not so friendly after my answer, though.

I actually laughed—I was so sick of being asked this. My first words, in sum, were, "Well, that certainly is an uninteresting question." Then I tried to dismantle the nonthinking behind it, pointing out that there is no demonstrated link between viewing violence and behaving violently, and that there are plenty of other, mainstream, film (and TV) genres much more irresponsible in the depiction of their violence.

This question is asked too often, and it needs to be addressed in more detail.

First, society is not becoming more violent. In fact, this is one of the least violent eras in human history. In the United States, for instance, violent crime has been declining for more than two decades. Second, no one has ever legitimately shown that viewing violence makes one violent. No one. As simple as that. Not that social reformers have not tried to do so whenever we are faced with a violent event, usually a mass shooting. The videogame lobby is now preparing itself for potential Congressional inquiry because a deranged homicidal man happened to play some of its violent games, even though many millions of other people do so every day without being driven to homicide. (If violence and videogames were linked, the top game-enthusiast countries of South Korea and the Netherlands should be the world's murder capitals.)

As Ed Neal says, "Psychotic people were psychotic before they got to the film. Why aren't the Sonja Henie movies from the 1940s all responsible for every youth in America wanting to be a ballet figure skater, whether male or female? It's the same thing."

Last, there's the question of why critics are going after horror movies. These movies do not pretend that death is heroic. They do not pretend that it is not horrifying. They do not pretend that violence isn't bloody, grotesque, and painful. If anything, they likely would repel the viewer from violence.

So even if, against evidence and reason, you still contend viewing violence leads to violence, why not go after the less responsible forms of violent entertainment, westerns or cop thrillers that feature numerous, nearly bloodless kills? Or, conversely, fault a film like the PG-rated *Raiders of the Lost Ark* (1981), which brings graphic face-melting gore directly to an audience of children? (I love the movie, myself.)

That is a real issue here. People go after *Chain Saw* and movies like it because these movies are easy targets for their anxieties. Other movies tend to present violence in a moral framework that makes it acceptable—death comes to the deserving. Horror movies, on the other hand, can feel threatening because their very stories and dynamics threaten moral frameworks—it is what they do to get under our skin—and so it is their very nature, then, that makes people uneasy and makes these movies such easy targets. If you're inclined to outrage, no need to think any further than that, really—just rant about the wrong things.

(About the question of responsibility, I think filmmakers' only obligation to the public is to deliver what they promise. If they deliver on that promise, they likely will have an audience. If they do not deliver, their audience will quickly fade away. But moral responsibility doesn't lie with the filmmaker, writer, artist, or dancer: it lies with the audience—or their parents.)

The trouble is that these questions and this attitude go well beyond some concerned concertgoer or professor and serve to rile up people in power. Every few years some television network gets in a twist about the corruption of children's minds and does a "special" about this issue—always rehashing the same tired ideas but with that year's latest threat (Marilyn Manson, *Grand Theft Auto*, *Natural Born Killers* . . .). To lead the audience to the right kind of concern, they often use *Chain Saw* as an example of something *really dangerous*. It hardly matters whether the movie is relevant to the particular point being made—the title alone is enough to frighten parents.

Then, of course, there are the self-appointed critics crusading against something they know nothing about. A telling case was Senator Paul Simon's 1990s campaign to rein in television violence. This crusade was inspired, he said, by seeing *The Texas Chain Saw Massacre* on a hotel TV one night in 1985. "I'm old enough to know it's not real, but is still bothered me that night," he said of that experience.

Horrible. Of course *Chain Saw* had not made it to TV in 1985 and would not even reach satellite or cable for another quarter century. It still is not on broadcast television, for obvious reasons. (That, of course, was a big joke on the set. This movie, we kept saying, would never be on TV. But times change.) So Senator Simon could not have seen it on TV. Nor could any of those innocent, unsuspecting children who might otherwise have been twisted by the experience. Maybe he had been watching a porn channel, and, like Stephen Koch, had confused pornography with violence.

Once again, the name *The Texas Chain Saw Massacre* was enough to invoke all the terrors adults have for their children's mental health (thank you, Warren Skaaren).

This misdirected concern for children's well-being and the public desire to protect them is not a new fight. In fact, it is a hollow echo of the 1950s campaign in the United States to censor—or simply shut down—"crime comics," a generic name that included war, horror, and any other violent context. Apparently these comics were very upsetting to children and were directly responsible for juvenile delinquency. (Originally a "juvenile delinquent" was just a kid who skipped school, but through some sinister 1950s mutation, the phrase came to evoke images of cigarette-smoking, motorcycle-riding, blue-jeans-wearing, switch-blade-switching, sneering teenage disrespect for all that was decent.)

Heading this campaign was psychiatrist Fredric Wertham, whose concerns began in the early 1940s through his work with juvenile delinquents. Almost all of them had read crime comics, and so Wertham concluded that these crime comics had contributed significantly to these juveniles' delinquency. (In a similar logical blunder, one might conclude that because all those who climb mountains breathe air, then surely breathing air causes mountain climbing.)

Wertham's campaign climaxed with his 1954 book, *Seduction of the Innocent*, an hysterical work that claimed that most comics were "lurid stories of crime, vice, lust, and horror." As a result, as writer Dwight Decker compactly summarizes Wertham, these comics "taught children to be cruel, sexually warped, dishonest, and contemptuous of soft virtues like pity or love." Upon reading, the book seems vaguely dismissive of psychology. It is also full of disturbing stories of violent teenagers, irresponsible parents, and frustrated judges conveniently wrought to make Wertham's points. Except that these stories are suspiciously generic and lacking in specifics, so there is no way to know whether any of them, or even any part of them, are true.

Sadly, few at the time seemed to notice either the extent to which Wertham's "evidence" was undocumented or the silliness of his argument. Concerned parents ate it up, as did Tennessee Senator Estes Kefauver, whose Senate Subcommittee on Juvenile Delinquency gave Wertham a national stage to call for legislation to stop the sale of comics to children under fifteen. After three days of hearings, the committee "suggested" to the comics publishers that "a competent job of self-policing within the industry will achieve much."

So, fearing direct government censorship, the publishers decided to censor themselves, creating the Comics Code. Wertham, of course, claimed he had not wanted censorship, though in the same breath he said that the new code was inadequate.

Whatever his claim, this was censorship. And it was effective. Crime comics died, along with many of their publishers and distributors. Horror comics (our major concern here) and their brutality and lurid art were gone—all the result of a misdirected concern about the corruption of children and a string of logical missteps.

But this is an old fight. It goes back, in a way, to Plato and his student Aristotle. They did not agree on many things, including the cathartic value of art. Plato feared that depictions of anti-social behavior were dangerous, because they stimulated our baser emotions and instincts. This pretty much is the same claim that critics of horror and violent film make today. Aristotle, on the other hand, said that art should not be censored, because it created emotions in its audience that helps keep them from needing to act out any dangerous desires. This is the very opposite of where most these critics stand. And that, in miniature, is the conflict that we have been acting out ever since.

That urge to censor has continued to this day, and seems especially keen in relation to *The Texas Chain Saw Massacre*.

It is a movie that, at one time or another, has been banned in Singapore, Chile, Brazil, Iceland, Finland, Norway, Ireland, West Germany—even in Sweden and France (for five years), both countries Americans tend to think of as liberal when it comes to these things. Maybe the most egregious example has been in England, where the national British Board of Film Censors refused to give *Chain Saw* permission to be shown when it was released in 1974. A local administration could issue its own license, which the Greater London Council did, allowing the movie to play in London theaters a short while on its initial release. It would take a quarter century for the Board to change its mind.

In the late 1990s, during the campaign to finally license *Chain Saw*, I went to a number of screenings at private film clubs across England, including England's prestigious National Museum of Photography, Film, and Television. There was a certain irony in watching *Chain Saw* at the museum while it was still banned from public viewing. (Presumably, it could be watched at these high cultural private screenings because members were sophisticated enough to not become violent.)

James Ferman, the head of the Board of Film Censors, inadvertently ended *Chain Saw*'s banishment—and likely his own career—in his response to this pressure regarding *Chain Saw*. Speaking to members of the British Film Institute after a screening of the movie at the 42nd London Film Festival in 1998, he said, "It's all right for you middle-class cineastes to see this film, but what would happen if a factory worker in Manchester happened to see it?"

That did it. The embarrassment to the Board was deep. Ferman retired soon after that, and the Board changed its name to the British Board of Film Classification, omitting the word "censor." *Chain Saw* was licensed and given a formal BBFC-18 (adults-only, rather than the more restrictive R18) rating. The Board said in a statement: "There is, so far as the Board is aware, no evidence that harm has ever arisen as a consequence of viewing the film." They also noted, "It is worth emphasizing that there is no explicit sexual element in the film and relatively little visible violence."

And then, in October 2000, *Chain Saw* was shown on British television's Channel Four. At the time the screening was announced, a spokesman said, "*The Texas Chain Saw Massacre* is a classic of the horror genre."

What were the censors so afraid of? What was it about horror movies that these people wanted to suppress? And why do critics go after horror movies whenever they want people to worry about the national psyche?

As a result of this attitude we are constantly asked to justify horror. Doug Bradley says, "If I am asked the question, 'Why horror?' I throw it back, and I ask, 'Why comedy?' which floors people, because comedy apparently doesn't need any justification. Why do we like comedy? Because it's funny and that apparently is all the explanation we need. So why horror? Because it's scary, because it's nasty, because it's unsettling, because it's disturbing. So that should be enough reason."

This answer is a key to the inverse question of why so many critics hate horror movies, and why government agencies and private citizens over the years have worked to remove horror from our lives.

Why do people hate *Chain Saw*? Because most of us respond to something nasty, unsettling, and disturbing by pushing it away, pretending it does not frighten us, pretending everything is okay.

Which it is not.

CHAPTER 18

OH, LEATHERFACE, I HOPE THAT'S NOT YOU

After Chain Saw's release I moved to New England and continued writing. I did make one more movie, the incomparably clumsy *The Demon Lover*, shot in the Detroit area. It was here that I learned what truly incompetent filmmaking is. I was also not paid. I had further dealings with a couple of producers who wanted to "help" my career. One day one of them justified his rudeness to a waitress at dinner by telling me that she was "just a robot" not worth bothering with. I told him I would not do business with him, and walked out of the restaurant. I did not want to be like these people, and I feared that I might become one of them.

Then I got a call from Bob Burns, our *Chain Saw* art director. He was in Los Angeles, working on another horror movie. The director was somebody no one had heard of, he said—Wes Craven. (Though of course by this point he had already made his notorious 1972 movie *The Last House on the Left*.) This movie was called *The Hills Have Eyes*, and there was a part for me as one of the killers. Could I be in Los Angeles in two weeks?

I said no. After my recent experiences, I was done with the movie business. Besides, I did not want to get sidetracked from writing.

It was the work I really wanted to do, and I knew I had to start doing it for a living. In fact, I was already looking for magazine assignments. I certainly was not interested in moving to the West Coast to work odd jobs while I chased a movie career. (Of course, I was not being asked to Suffer for Art. I was being asked to work on a movie. Somehow I could not see the difference.)

Anyway, I said no.

I stayed away from movies for more than a decade.

Then, in late December of 1986, I was in Paris on business. After getting drunk on too much good wine, I headed back to my hotel, where I threw myself on my bed. I hit the TV remote and there on the screen in front of my befuddled eyes appeared *The Texas Chain Saw Massacre*, in French. At least they had not needed to dub any of my lines. I did not watch long enough to see whether the good parts had been cut.

I really did not understand the significance of this—it just seemed odd and amusing at the time. Then one day a few months later a friend called to ask whether I would come out to L.A. for a long weekend to be in a little movie he was shooting. It was called *Hollywood Chainsaw Hookers*. He was calling it that, he said, because the word "massacre" was getting a bit overused.

I hesitated. And then I realized how stupid I had been earlier to turn down work.

So I said yes.

At that point something changed. On my second day of filming one of the actresses came up to me and said, "You know, you're a nice guy." Oh? Why would I be otherwise? "You're so famous that we all figured you were an asshole."

A light came on. This was why everyone had kept their distance my first day of filming. This was why no one on the crew had been willing to pick me up at the airport.

I started looking around. Our little chain saw movie was everywhere. There was even a *Texas Chain Saw Massacre* video game. I noticed a spate of movies with "massacre" in their titles—

Meatcleaver Massacre (1977), *Slumber Party Massacre* (1982), *Microwave Massacre* (1983), *Zombie Island Massacre* (1984), *The Nail Gun Massacre* (1985), *Mountaintop Motel Massacre* (1986) . . . the list goes on—and various inappropriate power tools in their plots. That was why it had been playing in Paris.

The Texas Chain Saw Massacre was big.

Then one night about this time, I was watching an episode of *Cheers*. Kirstie Alley's character, Rebecca, is lording it over everyone at the bar because she has been asked to house-sit an estate in the country over the weekend. In the last act, she is finally at the house—and scared about being alone. She locks the doors and windows, then cowers in the living room. She hears a noise and says, "Oh, Leatherface, I hope that's not you."

There was no explanation of who Leatherface was or what movie he was from.

Leatherface himself had entered the culture. So much so, in fact, that he was turning up everywhere. He was popping up in cartoons lampooning everything from domestic life (Wife on couch to chain-saw-wielding masked man: "Oh, please, Cedric. Must you turn every argument we have into a psychodrama?") to taxes (Man commenting on chain-saw-wielding masked man chasing woman: "Maybe it is time to reform the way the IRS does things."). In fact, Leatherface eventually made it to the November 1, 2010, cover of *The New Yorker*, appearing amid other iconic Halloween costume figures, including Superman, Batman, Robin, and Wonder Woman.

And now we had all sorts of masked characters wandering the streets of movie suburbia killing teenagers, albeit not with chain saws. (Though Tony Montana and his "little frien'" had by then also contributed to chain saw lore in 1983 in *Scarface*.) Never again would a chain saw be just a chain saw. I wondered if I should do a McCulloch (okay, Poulan) commercial.

Suddenly, I was visible. I had been, it seemed, some kind of enigmatic hermit who had disappeared into the North Woods to build stone houses and write haiku, as some horror fans apparently believed. But now, because of *Hookers,* I was back among the living. People started calling. They were calling for interviews. They were calling to invite me to horror fan conventions. They were calling about movie roles—though these calls always seemed to be more talk than actual movie making.

Public opinion of *Chain Saw* had evolved. It was showing up at film festivals, even winning now and then. People liked *The Texas Chain Saw Massacre.*

Even critics liked it and were saying good things. (Or some of them—plenty still hate the movie and what it stands for, whatever that is.)

In the *Village Voice,* Michael Goodman wrote, "*Chain Saw* captures the syntax and structure of a nightmare with astonishing fidelity. The quality of the images, the texture of the sound, the illogic by which one incident follows another—all conform to the way we dream. . . . What makes *Chain Saw* interesting is that since we are watching with our eyes open, it's a nightmare from which we can't wake up."

Lew Brighton, writing in *Film Journal,* called *Chain Saw* "the *Gone with the Wind* of meat movies." Allen Danziger says of *Chain Saw,* "It's no *Gone with the Wind.*" Bill Vale, describing his disappointment at first seeing it, says, "I don't know what I had expected, *Gone with the Wind*? I don't know what I was expecting, but what I got wasn't it." The wonderful irony here? The cans containing the original footage from *The Texas Chain Saw Massacre,* when I saw them in the University of Texas Film Collection, were sitting on a shelf next to the original footage of *Gone with the Wind.*

Academics were writing journal articles about *Chain Saw,* and then entire books about the once disdained horror genre, devoting chapters to *Chain Saw*'s meanings and significance. Christopher Sharrett, writing in *Planks of Reason: Essays on the Horror Film* in 1984, said that *Chain Saw* "represents a crucial moment in the history of the horror genre." Daryl Jones, writing in *Horror: A*

Thematic History in Fiction and Film in 2002, said that it was "the greatest of all horror movies." In 1992, U.C. Berkeley professor Carol Clover would publish the book *Men, Women, and Chain Saws: Gender in the Modern Horror Film* (with Leatherface on the cover), which would, among other things, coin the term for and introduce the concept of the "final girl," the ultimate survivor and focus of audience identification in numerous horror movies.

By 2005, Britain's *Total Film* magazine was also judging it the greatest of all horror movies, beating out my favorite, number sixteen, *The Haunting* (1963). Even more amazing to me, *Total Film* also said that *Chain Saw* was the nineteenth greatest movie of all time of any genre, coming in right before *Apocalypse Now* (1979) and right after *All About Eve* (1950). (I make none of these claims, myself. I only report.)

As its reputation grew, more people would cite some connection with the movie.

I discovered that apparently I had appeared as Leatherface at a child's third birthday party. Bob Burns brought me. Writer Harry Knowles wrote about my visit on his website, Ain't It Cool News, on June 2, 2004. He clearly remembered being in his red high chair in front of the dining table, on top of which sat a cake decorated with Godzilla eating his parents. Then the front door "blew open, and a sound of a chain saw filled the house." I came thundering in in full regalia, carrying a roaring chain saw. Bob followed behind, with a basket full of body-part props from the movie. Bob then gave the child his pick of one of the props—a hand, which Harry says can be seen briefly in the movie. (In a 2009 note referring back to the post, he added that Burns and I had come directly from wrapping *Chain Saw*, and that Bob gave him a toy saw.)

But of course, I was never at this party. Outside of the movie, I have never appeared anywhere in the Leatherface getup. Nor would I ever want to. Had someone else crashed Harry's party dressed as Leatherface?

As time went by, the connections to the film itself became even more direct. At first people were telling me that they knew someone who had worked on the movie. Then they started saying they had worked on the movie themselves, even though we had a core crew of about ten to fifteen. I had no idea who these people were, but there were more than fifteen of them.

The most shameless claim came when I was making an appearance back in Austin. A guy maybe in his mid-twenties came up to me with his date and said, "Hi. Remember me?"

I was puzzled. "No . . ." I said tentatively.

"Hondo, Texas, 1983."

"I've never been to Hondo."

"We worked on a movie there in 1983."

I tried to smile as I denied it. I had never been to Hondo. I had not worked on a movie in 1983. And I certainly had not made a movie in Hondo in 1983.

He frowned. "Oh, I see. And now I bet you're going to say you don't even remember me from *Chain Saw*."

I was too puzzled to even answer.

"I worked on *Chain Saw*! I was on the crew!" He sounded a bit irritated that I did not remember.

I looked at him and at his date. Then I understood. I imagined the scene: He had told her he worked in the movies. And as the story grew over time, he told her that he had worked on *Chain Saw*. So, when she saw that I was coming to town, she likely suggested they go say hello to his old friend Gunnar. I wanted to believe that she knew just what she was doing.

And, I imagined, he had decided to bluff his way through this.

I looked at them again.

"Listen," I said. "We made that movie before you were born."

He had not labored and suffered through that experience. He had not earned the right to make that claim. And he would not get a pass just because he was trying to impress his date. Life can be cruel.

Aside from this urge for personal involvement, people just wanted to talk about the movie, and their questions were often revealing about the movie and about the fans themselves. They talked about details of the movie, about the shooting, and about the other actors. Mostly they wanted to tell me stories of the first time they saw *Chain Saw*, or how it had made them lifelong horror fans. One told me that *The Texas Chain Saw Massacre* became his favorite movie five years before he ever saw it—just hearing the title had convinced him. Some fans were so affected by the movie that they named their children after me. These fans were almost always thoughtful about the movie and delighted to meet me. And I was delighted to meet them.

One question I heard often was some variant of "Who would win, Leatherface or Jason?" It always took me aback. At first I would answer with something like, "These are made-up characters. Whomever the writer wants to win will win." The response always was, "Yeah, but, really, who would win?"

There was actually something substantial behind the question. It revealed how deeply real Leatherface had become, psychologically. For fans, he existed outside the movie.

But some people, it turned out, believed that Leatherface was also physically real, that he existed in the flesh. One day someone said to me, "I knew the original Leatherface."

I said, "I am the original Leatherface, and I don't know you."

"Not the actor," he said, "the *guy*. Leatherface."

He claimed to have been a guard at the state prison in Huntsville, Texas. And Leatherface—the *real* one—he said, had been a prisoner there. Leatherface was so dangerous, he said, that if you showed him a picture of a chain saw he would go crazy.

Apparently he was not the only Texas prison guard who had met Leatherface. The next one told me that "they" had found that Leatherface had a lead imbalance in his brain. Once they fixed that, he was fine. In fact, he was working in the prison kitchen.

The topper came when I made an appearance at a fan convention in Niagara Falls, New York. One of the show's staff picked me up at the airport. On the way to the hotel she said, "You know, the original Leatherface lives right here in Niagara Falls. It's too bad we couldn't get him. It would have been great to have him at the convention with you." Yeah, really great.

I am not alone in this. Kim Henkel has run into it a few times. "I was in a bar in Houston one time," he says, "and somebody was telling me, not knowing the connection, that Leatherface was indeed incarcerated at Huntsville, and that he knew this for a fact because a family member was incarcerated there, and things like that. I wonder how many real Leatherfaces there are hanging out up there."

Maybe this is all because at the end of the movie Leatherface is still at large.

We laugh, but this notion of the real Leatherface is now so widespread that the Texas Prison Museum has felt compelled to say on its website that Leatherface is not and never was a prisoner in Huntsville, and that, indeed, he does not exist:

> With the recent release of the remake of the 1974 movie *Texas Chainsaw Massacre*, a lot of our patrons are asking about the murderer. They want to know if we have anything on the murderer, "Leatherface." What prison unit was he assigned to? How many people did he really kill? Did he kill anyone while in prison? When the first version of the movie came out, inmates in the Texas Department of Corrections became convinced that Leatherface was a particular inmate assigned to the Huntsville "Walls" Unit. Even today, some people are not completely convinced of the inaccuracy of this belief.

Tied to this belief in the truth of it all is people's goofy conviction that they actually know when and where it happened. Many claim to remember it. I often hear, "It happened in Corsicana. It was in all the papers. It was really scary." Over time, of course, the story has modified to, "My mother remembers when it happened. It was in all the papers. It was really scary." Corsicana, by the way, is not

later, in *The Odyssey*, Odysseus travels to the dark land of Erebus, a place filled with ghosts to whom he offers blood. In fact, Greek and Roman theater was often inhabited by masked demons and evil spirits.

In the Middle Ages, Europeans feared the possessed and the undead—werewolves, vampires, witches, and worse. These horrific creatures addressed something primal. Such stories continued well into more modern times as folk tales. As one scholar has said, "What is 'Little Red Riding Hood' but a werewolf story?"

Some dismiss the notion of these early origins for horror. They say that horror began with the Gothic tale, which developed in England and Germany in the mid-eighteenth century. But this seems to miss the point—Gothic tales are a literary genre, and horror is more than that. It is also an emotion, a relationship to the outside world of awe and fear of the unexplained and unknowable. Still, the Gothic tale is a kind of coalescing of these earlier horrific threads into a literary form of its own, and, as such, the Gothic tale is a large step in the development of the horror movie.

Of course, Gothic literature has nothing to do with the Goths. But it does present a fictionalized earlier time that is mysterious and dark. A Gothic tale is about its setting, often a castle or an abandoned ruin—a dark, old place. Here family secrets from the past haunt the characters of the story and offer a growing mood of foreboding. The story often centers on a creepy character who likely is a restless spirit or is risen from the dead or is some other undying monster. This monster—or the dark secret—threatens normalcy, destroying order and sanity. These stories are really about the haunted psyche, about paranoia and fear and about creating fear. In a way the purpose of the Gothic tale is titillation, to give the reader the shivers.

Horace Walpole's 1864 *The Castle of Otranto* is considered by most as the first English Gothic tale. Many others followed, including, of course, Mary Shelley's 1818 *Frankenstein*, which she started writing in 1816 at age eighteen in competition with friends to write a Gothic story. (The others were Lord Byron, Mary's husband-to-be Percy Shelley, and John Polidori, whose resulting 1819 short story, "The Vampyre," is considered the first Gothic vampire tale.) Of her effort, Shelley wrote, "I busied myself to think of a story, which would speak to the mysterious fears of our nature and awaken thrilling horror. One to make the reader dread to look around, to curdle the blood, and quicken the beating of the heart." Almost eighty years later, in 1897, Bram Stoker would publish *Dracula*.

The Gothic tale arrived during the Enlightenment and at the beginnings of the Romantic movement in art and literature. Some argue that the Romantic movement—and the Gothic—developed in reaction to the Enlightenment, which valued skepticism, observation, and rational thought over superstition and belief in the supernatural. Indeed, according to Enlightenment thinkers, there was nothing unknown or unknowable within the human psyche.

The Romantic, on the other hand, valued intuition and emotion, especially terror and horror in the face of nature, and embraced the exotic, a perfect breeding ground for the Gothic tale. The Romantic period itself saw a large shift in art and literature away from classical forms and toward the individual, the hero, and his or her reaction to the outside world. It became okay to look inside at our workings. Eventually we began to look at the underlayment of the mind itself.

It is no coincidence that after this, Sigmund Freud started to develop his ideas of the unconscious mind and ultimately his concept of the Uncanny and the return of the Repressed—that is, the return of those elements inside us which have always been there but which we have pushed away. Some believe, in fact, that Freud got his ideas of the Uncanny and the Repressed from the Gothic tale.

Both of these ideas tie closely to the Gothic and to horror. The Uncanny was the inexplicable and irrational in life. Freud characterized it as that which "arouses dread and horror . . .

certain things which lie within the class of what is frightening." He included the concepts of the demonic, gruesome, and dangerous. *Unheimlich*, the German word for the Uncanny, literally meant "un-homey" and implied, Freud said, that something uncanny might have once been familiar or at least secretly familiar.

Freud's concepts of the Repressed and the return of the Repressed follow from this. Childhood and adult traumas and conflicts are never resolved, he said. Instead they can fester in the unconscious and return as neurotic behaviors and phobias—or worse. We often call this repressed part of ourselves the Other. This ties closely to an element in the Gothic tale, that inside the antique house are monsters out of the past that will return. And then all hell will break loose.

Carl Jung did not quite agree with his teacher Freud about the Uncanny. He, instead, believed in the collective unconscious, the common experience and psychological grounding shared by all people. This unconscious was also the basis of the Shadow, he said, that part of the psyche that follows us, growing bigger and more demanding as we ignore it. It is dangerous and disorderly and always out of the field of vision. Of the Shadow, Jung said, "We have in all naïveté forgotten that beneath our world of reason another world lies buried." The Shadow was that thing that a person does not want to be, a close cousin to Freud's Repressed. At a personal level, the Shadow was the Other in us, Jung said. The collective Shadow was human evil.

This is rich ground for understanding horror. In a way, Dracula and Frankenstein's monster are both Freud's Repressed, or, if you prefer, Jung's Shadow. (As is Moby Dick, for that matter.) These two characters, now our most emblematic monsters, really marked the beginnings of the horror movie, with Edison's 1910 *Frankenstein* and Murnau's 1922 expressionist nightmare *Nosferatu*, a veiled version of Stoker's *Dracula*. Still, it was not until 1931, with the release of Todd Browning's *Dracula* and James Whale's *Frankenstein*, that these kinds of movies started being called horror.

There are differences between horror movies and Gothic tales, the most important being that the Gothic focuses on the setting—the dark, crumbling castle—while horror is more about fright. But both Gothic and horror do share elements, particularly the Repressed and the Shadow.

Horror movies go beyond that, of course. Some critics point out the dreamlike quality of film—that films represent the collective dreams of their audiences. In that context, horror turns that dream into a nightmare. If dreams are the doorway to the Shadow, maybe the nightmare lets that Shadow loose to roam freely. To Robin Wood (the first film scholar, I believe, to take *Chain Saw* seriously), this is the definition of the horror film—it is our collective nightmare. Another way to put this, Wood says, is that "normality is threatened by the Monster," and it is this relationship "that constitutes the essential subject of the horror film." Wood also says of *Chain Saw* that "beyond any other film in my experience" it possesses "the authentic quality of nightmare."

And of course, that brings us to the monster. Almost all horror movies have a monster. (*Jacob's Ladder* [1990], one of my favorites, seems not to.) And few horror movies have completely unsympathetic monsters. (Okay, nobody feels much for the Blob.) In many films the monster is the emotional center—the story really pivots around it—and often it is much more interesting than the victims, or the hero.

The monster also violates nature in some way. At some level it is seen as unstoppable. It has generally been considered supernatural, or at least beyond our reckoning. But this is not necessary—more and more, it seems, our monsters are physical and definitely of this world, a new idea in horror movies.

But what the monster represents is much bigger than the distinctions between supernatural and natural. Psychologically, it is beyond the normal and in some way bigger than existence. Horror does not have to be supernatural, but it must present what is unspeakable, beyond human understanding or experience.

Shortly after *Chain Saw*'s release, Tobe Hooper said, "The real monster is death." And though many, including Stuart Gordon, agree, I do not. The basic fear—the monster—within horror may be of death. But the horror goes beyond that. It can be existence itself. Or it can be more than death in some way—even the lack of death or maybe the *idea* of death, the infinitude after it. As told four thousand years ago, it was the realization of the *existence* of death that horrified Gilgamesh. Or we can take a cue from H. P. Lovecraft, the master of supernatural horror: horror could be cosmic awe and dread, the sense of the darkness within the universe that extends beyond death, ". . . a subtle attitude of awed listening, as if for the beating of black wings or the scratching of outside shapes on the known universe's utmost rim."

Whatever its elements, though, the horror movie is not, I think, defined by its overt content—the supernatural, monsters, darkness, whatever—but by the viewer's emotional reaction to what the movie creates. When horror works, you walk out of the theater feeling oppressed and empty, feeling as if you have glimpsed something that you did not want to see.

What is that horror feeling? To answer that, we have to start by looking at the difference between terror and horror, which are closely related. Terror is a kind of suspense or extreme fear. Horror, on the other hand, is about the larger meanings of what we are fearing. Michael Powell's *Peeping Tom* (1960) reveals, perhaps, that difference. The murderer Mark Lewis's victim feels terror—extreme fear. Through Lewis's lens, we in the audience watch as she realizes what is happening and is dying. In seeing that, we feel horror. We realize the implications of the killing we are seeing through her eyes.

Facing death brings terror; confronting the implications of death brings horror. My first experience of horror came when, at age eight or nine, I watched my brother in a play about a man in limbo, deciding whether to allow himself to die or to go back to life. When I left the theater I could not shake the feeling of soul-killing depression. This horror reaction is revulsion at what one faces. It is emotionally and psychologically—but not necessarily factually—true. Fears of monsters are larger and deeper than day-to-day fears. Sometimes the creature literally swims up from the darkness at the bottom of the sea—but it always does so psychologically.

"Horror is all about life and death and reincarnation and resurrection, damnation and expurgation, and the flesh and blood, all those big issues," Doug Bradley says. "Horror is the only genre where you can address that. It's the only genre that allows metaphysical speculation. The horror is the darkness, is the disturbing ideas that stay in your head and won't go away. People run away from it like people shouldn't have nightmares: it's bad to have nightmares. No, nightmares are good. Bring on the nightmares."

This is also a key to why so many critics hate real horror movies. *Peeping Tom* hit a nerve—maybe from carrying us too far into the horror. It was so disturbing, in fact, that it effectively ended Michael Powell's career in England. But horror movies, good ones anyway, are supposed to make us uncomfortable. They lift the curtain—just a little bit—of those deep psychological fears present at the beginning of consciousness. If we do not want to face those fears, if we want to pretend the Shadow does not exist, then we repress all that and the Shadow grows. As we push them away, they get stronger and we get angry when faced with them.

So, critics and many viewers get angry at horror movies and blame them for every wrong in our society. This anger likely is the key to censorship. Those who wish to censor movies do not believe that we must face darkness. Indeed, they believe it is a bad idea and it is a sin to let our children glimpse it. Isn't this why, in our child-"protecting" revised fairy tales, the wolf does not eat Little Red Riding Hood after all? Censors want to deny the existence of the dark side, the Shadow, of existence. When cave men sat around talking monsters, did someone scold them and say that this silly preoccupation would corrupt them and unnecessarily frighten the children? Likely they knew better.

But if horror is unpleasant at some level, why are people drawn to it? What do they get out of a horror movie? Of course, there is the argument based on Aristotle's idea of catharsis, of purification, that we go to horror movies because in our bland world we can feel threatened without real danger, we can climb aboard that roller coaster and feel fear, and then climb off unharmed. Then we go home to our safe beds, all the better for the experience.

But horror is more than just the scare. Again, this is the difference between terror and horror. If horror is about fear, it is about glimpsing what it is we fear—that is, gaining some small sense of what we fear, not just the feeling of fear itself. The reason for watching must be more deeply psychological than mere terror. As a child, I often had nightmares. But I discovered that when I went to bed, if I thought of the scariest thing I could imagine, the nightmares would not return that night. Horror resonates in our psyche. I think that, ultimately, horror's appeal is in the Shadow, in glimpsing the unfathomable, or some tiny part of it, of being reminded of the deep, unacknowledged parts of the human mind.

It is not pleasant, but it is necessary.

CHAPTER 20

A GRISLY WORK OF ART

Is *The Texas Chain Saw Massacre* a horror movie? One evening recently as I was having dinner with some friends in the horror business, one of them said to me, "Chain Saw isn't really a horror movie. To be horror, there has to be some supernatural element. Still, it's my favorite horror movie."

That pretty much answers it. Whether or not you believe that "real" horror must have a supernatural element, *Chain Saw* unquestionably evokes the emotions that define horror, that *are* horror—the sense of dread, oppression, and emptiness, the loss of control, the glimpse of the unfathomable.

Of course *Chain Saw* also has many of those story and character elements that most horror movies use to invoke these emotions—the monster and its centrality, the darkness (even in bright sunlight), the destruction of normality, the nightmare, the irrational, the gruesome and dangerous, evil.

It even has that Gothic essential, the old crumbling house in which the past looms. This time, though, it is the old Franklin place, and the past it carries is nothing more than Sally's recollections of zebras. The old house really is a bow to the

Gothic and an entry point into the nightmare.

Like the Gothic tale, from the beginning *Chain Saw* sets the mood of hostility and dread, with its gooey bodies and eerie flashes, close-ups of solar flares, lingering shots of the full moon, and the dead armadillo in the road. Over this we hear radio news reports about grave desecration in Muerto County, a refinery explosion in East Texas, a cholera epidemic in San Francisco, and a building collapse killing twenty-nine in Atlanta. There are outbreaks of violence, including attempted suicides in Houston. The bodies of a man and a woman with their features carved off and his genitals removed remain unidentified in Gary, Indiana. And in Dallas, an eighteen-month-old child had been found chained in an attic. This is not starting out to be a good day.

Inside the van, Pam reads the horoscope. Even the stars are out of kilter. Saturn is in retrograde. "When malefic planets are in retrograde—and Saturn is malefic—their maleficence is increased," she says. Something is terribly wrong here, and it's wrong on a cosmic scale.

Though the movie is firmly grounded in the physical world, these images and words hint at the supernatural, which Tobe Hooper might have made more overt with his "electronic being" in the chain saw family house had he and Kim Henkel not wisely replaced it with Leatherface.

And the foreboding continues right through the first act. At the old cemetery, the drunk sitting in the tire says, "I seen things. They say it's just an old man talking. You laugh at an old man. There's them that laughs and knows better." Strangers talking crazy are always a bad sign. Then the Hitchhiker, whom Franklin likens to Dracula, smears his own blood on the van as if some kind of hex. At the gas station the Cook warns them not to go to the old house. Once there, after Kirk sees the daddy longlegs swarming on the wall, Franklin spots the nest of bones and feathers on the floor, then sees the bone fetish hanging overhead. Very bad, indeed.

What are we being led into? What is *Chain Saw* about? At one level the answer is simple. When I am asked, I say it is about scaring the crap out of you. When I tell Kim this, he says, "Oh, yeah. Absolutely."

Daniel Pearl agrees. "To me it was about being scary and working at gut level more than a rational level," he says. "As a cinematographer that's sort of where I come from."

I think that is right. Scaring you is any horror movie's first responsibility, and that is the primary concern when writing, filming, and editing it. Without that, the rest matters little.

But *Chain Saw* is not just about scaring you. As Kim said earlier, while writing *Chain Saw* he thought of it as a kind of Hansel and Gretel story. From the beginning he thought of it as more than just the scare.

So, too, with Tobe. "When we were talking about the film, Tobe always considered it a political allegory and a comedy," Daniel says. "He would say that over and over again. This is a comedy, this is a political allegory. It was all about the gas shortage, the food shortage, and the shortages that were going to be coming about."

Of course, in looking at the final film, it is important to not let our knowledge of the writers' and director's intentions cloud our understanding of their creation. Putting aside Tobe's and Kim's early plans, what did we end up with?

When Kim looks at *Chain Saw* forty years on, he sees an interesting question. "What is an entity, an individual, a society entitled to do when they see that their way of life is threatened?" he says. "The conventional answer is, 'Well, you can kill 'em, but you can't eat 'em.' *Chain Saw* crosses the line, violates the taboo, and says, 'No, in defense of your position you may go that extra yard.' In essence, what they had encountered was an impediment to their way of life. So how do we respond? What are we entitled to do in responding to the risk that we're facing?"

We know that the members of the family were all slaughterhouse workers laid off when killing machines were brought in—virtually the only part of their background that is explained. In response, before our travelers ever arrive, the family has redirected these killing skills at people, whom they eat and sell as barbecue. What wonderful revenge, keeping themselves in groceries while also feeding like a succubus on the society that has discarded them.

With the arrival of our five victims, though, we have an added element, the problem of having one's home invaded by strangers. This must just add salt to the wound. No wonder Leatherface is so fussy after he dispatches Jerry—he wants to protect the family.

This puts the family, instead of the victims, at the center of the film. It would also explain why Tobe and Kim found the family members so much more interesting than the victims. But then, this is essential for horror movies—the monster is the center of the movie. In this case, as critic Robin Wood said, "The monster is the family." All this terror comes from within the family. They are the ones who threaten and destroy normality. They are the ones who bring on the nightmare.

And what is this family? "Probably the biggest thing that creeps people out when they first see this movie," Tim Harden says, "is how screwed-up this family is, but they think it's normal. They think nothing of it. It's just a family trying to get by."

A curious element here is the absence of women. The parents' generation is gone. More importantly, the mother is gone. Nor is there a grandmother, other than a desiccated corpse that keeps Grandpa company upstairs. None of this dynamic is explained, of course—we just come into the middle of it and see it as it is.

This absence means that the family is distorted—a pack of males lacking any balancing element, a parody of family life. Granted, Leatherface does try to add a female element by dressing up as the Old Lady while making dinner, and then later as the Pretty Woman at the "last supper." But he fails. Curiously, this male imbalance does not produce a kind of testosterone-driven sexuality. We are far past that. Instead, it is perverted into sadism and cannibalism.

These characters are atavistic. They are regressions into an earlier humanity, or subhumanity, where the pursuit of urges dominates. We see the conflict of this regression in the Cook, who seems to cling to fragments of his humanity before rejecting them. He tries erratically to impose order, but the bad-boy Hitchhiker will have none of it, while Leatherface just does what he is told.

Leatherface is a curious mix of brutality and power on the one hand, and fear and obedience on the other. He is also mysterious. He does not speak. We know nothing about him—how he got this way, or, for that matter, what is under the mask.

He is the monster, even without the family. "Leatherface was a monster without having to be created like a Frankenstein monster," Ted Nicolaou says. "He had all the appearance of the monster but was just something of this world, which was pretty shocking."

His mask—the blank behind the mask—brings the horror. It is the hidden, after all, that drives horror. With the monster featureless there is nothing there for his victim to negotiate with to try to survive. "Although there is humanity in there," Doug Bradley says, "it's shut off, it's closed, you can't access it."

The mask also makes us wonder whether Leatherface is the Shadow, the dark self that haunts all of us and which we can never quite see. If he were unmasked and seen, that identity with the dark self would be lost.

Leatherface's masks are also about performance. He changes them for each setting. They echo the shaman in the cave who puts on a mask to become a demon for a time. The mask continues in this sense into the more formalized theater of the Greeks, in which the mask both represents and is the character being portrayed. It is the same with Leatherface. Like the shaman and the actor, he calls up the demon. This is part of the appeal—and horror—of Leatherface.

Beyond the mask itself, apparently Leatherface makes curious forms of art. Remember the "grisly work of art" (as the newsman on the radio calls it) in the cemetery. Once home, he sets to decorating the house. "The skull furniture, almost like art pieces, which presumably had been created by Leatherface," Doug Bradley says, "that changes the whole perception because he's not just a big guy with a chain saw running around cutting people up. He's also an artist. And that's a difficult idea to throw in, but it makes him shamanic. And it's another element in the film where modern life is being confronted by what is older, deeper, darker."

Curiously, for all this darkness, Leatherface, like the Cook, is a bit sympathetic. Maybe it is because we glimpse a bit of his humanity in his scene at the window. Or maybe it is his desire to dress up to impress their dinner guest.

"You know how Lenny [in *Of Mice and Men*] kills the rabbit and then kills the girl?" John Landis says. "Absolutely, Lenny is a brute and a murderer, a killer, but he's not evil. And I don't think that Leatherface . . . he gets no glee out of it. He's doing work, and he's doing bidding, and he's doing what he's told, and he's also protective of the family."

There is more to him than just evil. And in that, we make him and all the family more complex, ambiguous, and compelling.

It also creates a conundrum for us. *Fangoria* journalist David Goodfellow said to me recently, "*Chain Saw* goes beyond the spider, beyond the thing that scares you. It goes into the darkness inside you—you have to ask yourself where you stand in all this. Do you sympathize with the victims, do you take the side of the killers? It goes under the stairs. And under the stairs there is a drain. And you go down that drain." As Kim said, the monster is us.

That considered, we still have the life-and-death conflict between the family and the hapless travelers, represented ultimately by the solitary Sally. We watch this family of friends slaughtered one by one, each death seemingly inevitable. Each time Sally escapes—first to the house, then to the gas station—she only returns to the horror. When she finally escapes to the road, it is hardly an escape. By now she is so damaged that she is done for.

"This girl's never going to be the same," Ed Neal says. "She's no longer even a human being. She's been reduced to that because of the intensity of the horrors she's been through. That doesn't have a denouement. She just goes bumping down the road screaming at the top of her lungs, beating on the side of the truck, and you don't know what happens to her. And the ambulance doesn't come, and the CSI people don't come and clean her up, and 'Everything's going to be okay, you're all right now.' There is none of that."

Somehow this is part of every urban dweller's rural nightmare, the unintended confrontation with insane, resentful country folk. "Everyone's probably secret terror is that they will walk through a door that will lead into a little pocket of hell and not come out," Ron Bozman says. "I think it was just the perfect depiction of people taking the wrong road, the classic horror formula. They took the wrong road, went into the wrong house, and only one of them survived. It just captured the horror of that predicament." Part of the strength of this movie is that it is not supernatural. It is believable. You walk out of the theater muttering, "There are people like this out there."

And all through this the audience feels like they are watching the real thing actually happening, that they are watching a documentary—thanks to *Chain Saw*'s budget limitations and to the decisions the filmmakers made about how they were going to shoot the movie. It is real to the audience, which also means that it seems to be happening to them—increasing its emotional power.

"You watch that movie and you think, *Anything can happen. I don't trust the director,*" John Landis says. "You don't consciously think that, and I think that's what *Chain Saw* very successfully does from the beginning of it, this ambience is set up where you think, *Who the fuck is making this movie?* It's not conscious. The audience doesn't literally think who the fuck's making the movie, but they're on guard. Because they really are in the hands of—the sense of crazy is very real in that movie."

So what is going on here? What is this movie about? Well, among other things, it is about the end of the world, the apocalypse. As we learn in the beginning, the stars are out of alignment and brutal random violence is spreading.

Critic Robin Wood has said that, in a way, *Chain Saw* shows the past devouring the present—and the younger generation. Shades of the Gothic, in which a dark secret from the past threatens to destroy the present. (This said, yes, it could also be about Viet Nam, as some have suggested, or about the gas shortage, as Tobe thought. Or it could even be about vegetarianism, I suppose. But I leave those interpretations to others.)

In most horror movies, evil is vanquished in the end and order is restored. But not in *The Texas Chain Saw Massacre*. "No, he doesn't go to jail," Ed says. "The police never come. They never come."

Sally escapes only with her life and nothing more. Everything else for her is destroyed. We are left watching a frustrated Leatherface dancing out his anger until everything goes black. That is the end of it.

The monster goes unpunished. He is still there, still capable of returning. The normality, the predictability of the world is gone. There is no punishment. There is no relief of suffering. There is no justice. There is no order. Without justice and order, how can we have meaning? It is all nothing.

This is the real horror.

———•———

The Texas Chain Saw Massacre changed horror movies. After Leatherface we had the onslaught of the masked killers, led by Jason Voorhees and Michael Myers. All these movies' killers used every power and hand tool imaginable to slaughter the innocent. The teenagers in the van became perennial, even to the point that there is almost always a Franklin, the fifth wheel who does not quite fit in with the others, usually two couples. The Franklin never survives.

And, of course, it was the forerunner of the "slew of hillbilly pointless violence movies," as Doug Bradley calls them. The redneck apocalypse, I suppose.

But more than these story details, it changed some basic elements of horror movies. Horror of the 1950s and '60s was moribund—bad sci-fi creature movies that pretended to be horror, or polite, unadventurous recreations of Poe tales. It was hard to call Roger Corman's 1963 *The Raven* horror, even though it was packed with our favorites—Vincent Price, Peter Lorre, and Boris Karloff. At best, it was irony.

Chain Saw, on the other hand, broke the rules, as did some before it, most notably *Psycho* and *Night of the Living Dead*. Before this, horror movies were polite. They took their time getting rolling, sometimes with a first act that was nothing but talk to set up the plot. The audience also knew when they were safe—a cut from the action to an office scene or other set piece would cue them. (Often this scene would be in Washington, D.C., with the Capitol Building in the background.) We knew that for a while we could relax and catch our collective breath.

Instead of the slow setup, *Chain Saw* creates a sense of dread from the very beginning, and once the Hitchhiker arrives, we know we are in for a wild ride. There is nothing safe about this movie. It quickly becomes a nightmare that does not end, even after the movie's last reel. And along the way it transforms our sense of the family as normality to the family as transgressor.

Most importantly, perhaps, *Chain Saw* changed something fundamental in horror—good no longer always overcomes evil. The monster was not destroyed. As an audience we were not safe in that respect, either. The movie was nihilistic, and it allowed many others after it to be.

"There are some people who will never like horror movies no matter what," Stuart Gordon says. "But I think what it was, was that it just really took horror to a new level, it really did. It was a groundbreaking movie."

People talk about *Chain Saw*'s being the original splatter movie and the foundation of torture porn. But *Chain Saw* is neither. Its blood is minimal, and death is treated almost indifferently. As to the torture porn part, maybe that is a reference to the dinner scene, in which the family torments Sally relentlessly—but again this is emotional torture. Maybe it is just the name. *The Texas Chain Saw Massacre*. It sounds bad.

Truthfully, I doubt that any of us ever thought *Chain Saw* would become what it has. "We all thought it was really potent, but [we] had no idea it would be as good [as it was] and have the impact that it had," Ron Bozman says. "It was total shock that it took off. Certainly none among us on Quick Hill Road would ever . . . in your wildest dreams, [we] could never have projected the impact this film would have, and the life, and the afterlife. Forty years later it's still in the conversation, it's still in the literature of film."

"Peter Bogdanovich said 'the only true test of a movie is time,'" John Landis says. "And there are many movies, giant hit movies—*The Greatest Show on Earth*, Best Picture [in 1952]. It's unwatchable, that movie. But when you see *Citizen Kane*, it is as thrilling as any of the great films. I really believe *Texas Chain Saw* is in there, I really think so."

But how did we get *this* movie? It was the script, the directing, the art directing, the cinematography and documentary feel, the sound design and score, and the editing. It was the family of monsters and this new monster, Leatherface. It was the acting. In fact it was all those things that the crew and cast brought to the film. And it was the small budget and its effects—the shortage of lights, the need to shoot in 16mm, the nonexistent special effects.

It was the heat, the smell, the impossible hours, the frenzy and insanity of shooting the dinner scene—the overall misery. It was the particular combination of actors and crew, most of whom had never made a movie and were willing to do whatever it took to get *Chain Saw* made. It was even the photo lab's sloppy work that produced the murky, off-color release prints. And it was the title.

Take away any of these parts and it would all fall down.

Somehow all these elements created something new and unexpected. Somehow, just for this one time, we caught lightning in a bottle.

The movie is what it is because of this combination—and because this time Saturn was not in retrograde.

ACKNOWLEDGMENTS

Four friends from *The Texas Chain Saw Massacre* are gone now.

Jim Siedow (6/12/1920–11/12/2003) was the real actor among us. He was such a kind man that it broke his heart when he had to hit Marilyn during the filming. In the years after the movie, I took great pleasure in visiting him and his wife, Ruth, in their amused retirement in Houston.

Bob Burns (5/27/1944–5/31/2004) was one of the most creative, generous, difficult, and kindhearted friends I ever had. When I was working on a book in Texas and needed a place to stay, he gave me his spare bedroom for six weeks.

Paul Partain (5/3/1946–1/27/2005) drove us all crazy with his whining during the shoot. I met him again some years later and discovered what a fine person he really was. We spent many evenings at his home outside Austin, eating spaghetti and sitting on his patio, telling lies.

Lou Perryman (8/15/41–4/1/2009) kept me sane during the filming, talking about philosophy and movies and whatever else was on our minds. Sadly, he died because he opened his door to help a stranger.

Many people gave long hours to talk with me about *Chain Saw*. And they were brave enough to do it in front of a microphone.

All the cast and virtually all the crew members that I was able to contact joined in enthusiastically to help make this book. I want to thank them for giving me so much of their time. Their memories of the filming and their insights into the movie after all these years were invaluable. My heartfelt thanks to Wayne Bell, Ron Bozman, Marilyn Burns, Larry Carroll, Mary Church, Allen Danziger, John Dugan, Ed Guinn, Kim Henkel, Teri McMinn, Ed Neal, Ted Nicolaou, Daniel Pearl, and Bill Vail. I am pleased that so many of us have remained friends.

In addition, Doug Bradley, Stuart Gordon, Tim Harden, John Landis, and Steph Sciullo let me interview them about their experiences with the movie and their thoughts about its place in horror. They all added significantly to this book. I particularly appreciate the years of talk with Doug.

My thanks to Richard Curtis, my literary agent, who liked this idea and sold it; to Steven Mockus, my editor at Chronicle Books, who liked this idea and bought it and then made it better; and to Mike Eisenstadt, my theatrical agent, who was the first to tell me he wanted to read this book.

Thank you to those who gave me access to *Chain Saw* photographs and helped me find more: Marilyn Burns, John Dugan, Michael Felsher, Tim Harden, Kim Henkel, Ken Kish, David Munoz, Daniel Pearl, and Desmond Root.

There are others. My thanks to Tippi Hedren for helping me get her bird story straight; writer Paolo Zelati for letting me use material from his unpublished 2008 interview with Tobe Hooper; writer Stefan Jaworzyn for a transcript of his interview of me for his *Texas Chain Saw Massacre Companion*; writer Mattias Lindeblad for a transcript of his interview of me for his book *Skräk*; writer Thomas Nilsson for information on film censorship in Sweden; Carl Mazzocone, producer of *Texas Chainsaw 3D*, for his efforts on my behalf; and Jean Fosillo for transcribing a hundred thousand words of interviews accurately and quickly, all the while seeming to enjoy it.

More personally, I thank Bill Kotzwinkle and Elizabeth Gundy for their conversations and early enthusiasm and for helping me make contact with the outside world.

And, most personally, I thank my partner, Betty Tower, who put up with my disappearances for days at a time, and my impossible schedule for months at a time. She bravely read the entire manuscript just to see if it made any sense and, in the process, saved me from submitting a book full of errors. (The ones that remain are all my doing, though I refuse to take any responsibility for them.)

She also reminded me that I once studied baton twirling, likely the key to my agile dancing with the chain saw.

SELECTED BIBLIOGRAPHY

Bradley, Doug. *Sacred Monsters: Behind the Mask of the Horror Actor*. London, UK: Titan Books, 1996.

Farley, Ellen, and William K. Knoedelseder, Jr. "The Real Texas Chain Saw Massacre." *Los Angeles Times Calendar* (September 5 & 12, 1982).

Goodwin, Michael. "A Real Nightmare Makes a Great Horror Film." *The Village Voice* (February 9, 1976).

Hardy, Phil, ed. *The Encyclopedia of Horror Movies*. New York, NY: Harper & Row, 1986.

Hogle, Jerrold E., ed. *The Cambridge Companion to Gothic Fiction*. Cambridge, UK: Cambridge University Press, 2002.

Iaccino, James F. *Psychological Reflections on Cinematic Terror: Jungian Archetypes in Horror Films*. Westport, CT: Praeger, 1994.

Jaworzyn, Stefan. *The Texas Chain Saw Massacre Companion*. London, UK: Titan Books, 2003.

Koch, Stephen. "Fashions in Pornography." *Harper's Magazine* (November, 1976).

Perry, Danny. *Cult Movies*. New York, NY: Dell Publishing, 1981.

Phillips, Kendall R. *Projected Fears: Horror Films and American Culture*. Westport, CT: Praeger, 2005.

Schneider, Kirk J. *Horror and the Holy*. Chicago, IL: Open Court, 1993.

Silver, Alain, and James Ursini. *Horror Film Reader*. New York, NY: Limelight Editions, 2000.

Trombetta, Jim. *The Horror! The Horror!: Comic Books the Government Didn't Want You to Read!*. New York, NY: Abrams, 2010.

Weaver, James B., and Ron Tamborini. *Horror Films: Current Research on Audience Preferences and Reactions*. Mahwah, NJ: Lawrence Erlbaum Associates, 1996.

Wood, Robin, et al. *American Nightmare: Essays on the Horror Film*. Toronto, ON: Festival of Festivals, 1979.

Worland, Rick. *The Horror Film: An Introduction*. Oxford, UK: Blackwell Publishing, 2007.

Zinoman, Jason. *Shock Value*. New York, NY: The Penguin Press, 2011.

INDEX